THE EUROPEAN CHALLENGE

✦

TIME ®
LIFE
BOOKS

Other Publications:

WEIGHT WATCHERS₈ SMART CHOICE RECIPE COLLECTION
TRUE CRIME
THE ART OF WOODWORKING
LOST CIVILIZATIONS
ECHOES OF GLORY
THE NEW FACE OF WAR
HOW THINGS WORK
WINGS OF WAR
CREATIVE EVERYDAY COOKING
COLLECTOR'S LIBRARY OF THE UNKNOWN
CLASSICS OF WORLD WAR II
TIME-LIFE LIBRARY OF CURIOUS AND UNUSUAL FACTS
AMERICAN COUNTRY
VOYAGE THROUGH THE UNIVERSE
THE THIRD REICH
THE TIME-LIFE GARDENER'S GUIDE
MYSTERIES OF THE UNKNOWN
TIME FRAME
FIX IT YOURSELF
FITNESS, HEALTH & NUTRITION
SUCCESSFUL PARENTING
HEALTHY HOME COOKING
UNDERSTANDING COMPUTERS
LIBRARY OF NATIONS
THE ENCHANTED WORLD
THE KODAK LIBRARY OF CREATIVE PHOTOGRAPHY
GREAT MEALS IN MINUTES
THE CIVIL WAR
PLANET EARTH
COLLECTOR'S LIBRARY OF THE CIVIL WAR
THE EPIC OF FLIGHT
THE GOOD COOK
WORLD WAR II
HOME REPAIR AND IMPROVEMENT
THE OLD WEST

*For information on and a full description of any of the
Time-Life Books series listed above, please call
1-800-621-7026 or write:*
Reader Information
Time-Life Customer Service
P.O. Box C-32068
Richmond, Virginia 23261-2068

This volume is one of a series that chronicles the history and culture of the Native Americans. Other books in the series include:

THE FIRST AMERICANS
THE SPIRIT WORLD
PEOPLE OF THE DESERT
THE WAY OF THE WARRIOR
THE BUFFALO HUNTERS

The Cover: A member of an Indian welcoming party offers fish to the crew of a French vessel exploring the southeast coast of North America in the 16th century. Native American peoples regarded gift giving as essential to good relations between households and tribes, and many freely extended that courtesy to the mysterious white men who descended on their shores.

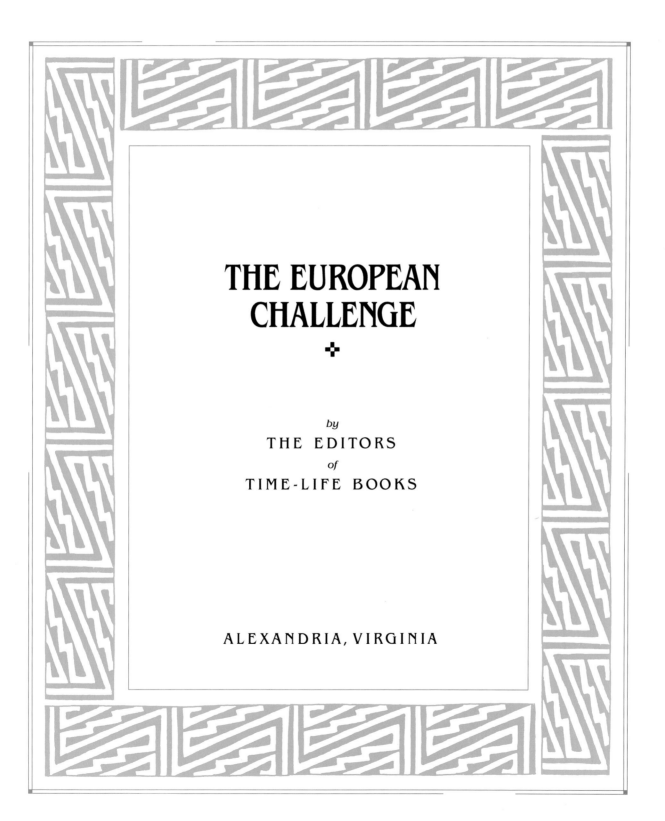

THE EUROPEAN CHALLENGE

✤

by
THE EDITORS
of
TIME-LIFE BOOKS

ALEXANDRIA, VIRGINIA

THE AMERICAN INDIANS

SERIES EDITOR: Henry Woodhead
Administrative Editor: Jane Edwin

Editorial Staff for *The European Challenge*
Art Directors: Herbert H. Quarmby (principal),
Dale Pollekoff
Picture Editor: Jane Coughran
Text Editors: Stephen G. Hyslop (principal),
John Newton
Writer: Maggie Debelius
Associate Editors/Research: Harris J. Andrews,
Mary Helena McCarthy (principals), Robin Currie,
Kirk E. Denkler
Assistant Editor/Research: Annette Scarpitta
Assistant Art Director: Susan M. Gibas
Senior Copyeditor: Ann Lee Bruen
Picture Coordinator: David Beard
Editorial Assistant: Gemma Villanueva

Special Contributors: Ronald H. Bailey, Charles S.
Clark, George Constable, George G. Daniels, Lydia
Preston, David S. Thomson (text); Martha Lee Beck-
ington (research); Barbara L. Klein (index).

Correspondents: Elisabeth Kraemer-Singh (Bonn),
Christine Hinze (London), Christina Lieberman
(New York), Maria Vincenza Aloisi (Paris), Ann
Natanson (Rome). Valuable assistance was also pro-
vided by: Janet Huseby (Berkeley); Barbara Gevene
Hertz (Copenhagen); Fran Gardner Youssef (Irvine);
Sarah Moule (London); Trini Bandrés (Madrid); Cathy
Booth (Miami); Glenn Mack, Aselle Sarina, Juan P.
Sosa (Moscow); Elizabeth Brown, Katheryn White
(New York); Ann Wise (Rome); Ana Martinez (Santo
Domingo); Carolyn L. Sackett (Seattle); Mary Johnson
(Stockholm).

General Consultants
Frederick E. Hoxie is director of the D'Arcy McNickle
Center for the History of the American Indian at the
Newberry Library in Chicago. Dr. Hoxie is the author
of *A Final Promise: The Campaign to Assimilate the
Indians 1880-1920* and other works. He has served
as a history consultant to the Cheyenne River and
Standing Rock Sioux tribes, Little Big Horn College
archives, and the Senate Select Committee on Indian
Affairs. He is a trustee of the National Museum of the
American Indian in Washington, D.C.

Neal Salisbury is Professor and Chair of the History
Department at Smith College in Northampton, Massachusetts. Throughout his career, he has specialized in
the study of Indians in colonial North America and
has written extensively about this subject. Among his
publications are *Manitou and Providence: Indians,
Europeans, and the Making of New England, 1500-
1643* and *The Indians of New England: A Critical Bib-
liography.* Dr. Salisbury has been a research fellow at
the Smithsonian Institution and the D'Arcy McNickle
Center for the History of the American Indian, and a
Fellow at the National Humanities Center. He is a
member of the American Historical Association, the
Organization of American Historians, and the American Society for Ethnohistory.

Special Consultants
Bill Holm, retired since 1985, was for many years Cu-
rator of Northwest Coast Indian Art at the Burke Museum in Seattle and a professor of art history at the
University of Washington. Drawing upon his longtime
interest and involvement in Native American cultures,
he is working on a series of acrylic paintings of the
people of the Plains, Plateau, and Northwest Coast.
Professor Holm has lectured widely on native Northwest arts and cultures and has published numerous
books, including *Northwest Coast Indian Art: An
Analysis of Form* and *Box of Daylight: Northwest
Coast Indian Art.*

Albert H. Schroeder spent more than 30 years with
the U.S. National Park Service until his retirement in
1976. During much of that time he was a southwest-
ern interpretive archaeologist with a special interest
in linking late prehistoric and early historic Indian
cultures. Mr. Schroeder has been a frequent contribu-
tor to numerous scholarly journals on the subject
of archaeological, ethnological, and early historical
research relating to the American Indians of the
Southwest.

Library of Congress Cataloging in Publication Data
The European challenge/by the editors of Time-
Life Books.
     p. cm. — (The American Indians)
   Includes bibliographical references and index.
   ISBN 0-8094-9408-6
   ISBN 0-8094-9409-4 (lib. bdg.)
     1. Indians of North America—First contact with
Europeans. 2. Indians of North America—His-
tory. 3. Indians of North America—Social condi-
tions. 4. Europe—Colonies—America. 5. Fron-
tier and pioneer life—United States—History.
   I. Time-Life Books. II. Series.
E98.F39E87 1992   92-1582
970.004'97—dc20   CIP

CONTENTS

1
THE FIRST ENCOUNTERS

2
CONFLICT IN THE NORTH WOODS

3
THE PLIGHT OF THE PUEBLOS

4
INTRUDERS ON PACIFIC SHORES

ESSAYS

1

THE FIRST ENCOUNTERS

A chief of Florida's Timucua Indians proudly shows the leader of a 1564 French expedition how his people worship at a stone marker erected by earlier French explorers, in this sole surviving painting by the expedition's artist, Jacques le Moyne. Some Native Americans initially regarded the Europeans as supernatural beings and cherished their gifts, such as the glass bead necklace shown at top.

Guacanagari was eager to meet the mysterious white visitor who called himself Colón. As one of several rival caciques, or chiefs, on the Caribbean island of Bohío, Guacanagari was ever alert to distinctions of rank, and he had reason to believe that Colón was an important man, and perhaps more. People were saying that Colón and the crews of his giant ships had come from the sky—the home of powerful spirits—and that they offered wondrous charms to those who paid them tribute in the form of gold.

For more than a week now, the Spanish vessels commanded by Colón—known to posterity as Columbus—had been besieged off the coast of this island he dubbed Hispaniola by hundreds of native peoples in canoes, who presented the visitors with bits of gold and colorful parrots, an honor reserved for exalted figures in their culture. In return, the islanders received glass beads and chiming ornaments they called *chuque chuque cascabeles,* brass bells that Europeans tied to the legs of hawks or falcons. A party of explorers from one of the ships had even gone ashore to visit Guacanagari's main village, Guarico, attracting a crowd of people who came to exchange gifts or simply to stare at these strange bearded men cloaked in cloth. The visitors in turn marveled at the islanders' smooth faces, long coarse hair, and unclad bodies.

Colón himself was anxious to meet Guacanagari, for he hoped to enlist his aid in locating sources of gold on the island. The opportunity came sooner than expected. On Christmas Eve, 1492, Columbus's flagship *Santa Maria* ran aground in shallows off the coast and split open. Fearing that all its provisions would be lost, he sent aides to Guarico seeking help. Guacanagari dispatched retainers to console Colón in the traditional local manner—by weeping for him. In a more practical gesture, he also sent a fleet of large dugout canoes, hewn from tree trunks, racing to the stricken ship. His men salvaged food and other cargo and shuttled it to storehouses in the village, completing the transfer, one early chronicler of the expedition noted admiringly, "without a needle missing."

As this incident underscored, the islanders possessed resources that were better suited to the demands of their environment, in some respects, than the elaborate contrivances of the Europeans. Plying their sturdy canoes, people who called themselves Taino—meaning "noble" or "prudent"—had pushed off boldly from the South American mainland more than 1,500 years before the time of Columbus to settle on Bohío and surrounding islands. Their descendants thrived in that tropical setting, raising cotton, tobacco, cassavas, and other root crops; crafting splendid objects of clay, wood, bone, and shell; and traveling from island to island in dugouts that carried up to 40 people in order to trade with neighbors. The Bohío residents were rich in ceremony and materially prosperous enough to maintain scores of villages, some with thousands of people. Columbus's men who visited Guarico praised its well-ordered streets and houses, arrayed around a central plaza that was "very well swept"—a tidy picture that compared favorably with the typical European village of the time.

Columbus's discoveries in the Caribbean, which included the large islands of Hispaniola and Cuba, are shown on the map above along with areas of North America explored and colonized by European expeditions that followed in the next century. The Spaniards penetrated the vast region they called Florida, reaching the Appalachian Mountains. French voyagers tried to settle near the Saint Johns River. The English landed farther north, at Roanoke Island on the Carolina coast, then at Jamestown in Virginia.

On the day after Christmas, having overseen the successful salvage operation, Guacanagari himself went out to the ship *Niña,* where Columbus and the crew from the *Santa Maria* were now quartered, to offer condolences and invite the admiral to his village. On reaching the town, Columbus presented the cacique with gloves and a blouse, emblems of wealth and dignity among the Europeans. In exchange, Guacanagari gave the admiral a carved mask with golden eyes and other glittering ornaments that signified authority among his people. Far from being cowed by this visitor from another world, Guacanagari was claiming a personal relationship with him as one chief to another. Columbus, for his part, was willing to humor the cacique, but he was also intent on proving his superiority. Aware that the locals were awestruck by Spanish weaponry, he had his men fire off a few rounds from two small cannon, sending the cacique and his people sprawling in terror.

Sadly, Columbus's intimidating show would set the tone for a new age of cultural confrontation. In this early meeting between Europeans and Native Americans, as in similar encounters to come, friendly overtures would soon give way to coercion. It mattered little where the intruders came from or what they sought—whether they were Spanish soldiers and priests pursuing mineral wealth and converts from the Caribbean to California, English settlers carving out plantations in the forests of Virginia and Massachusetts, Frenchmen pursuing the fur trade in the Canadian interior, or Russian merchants plying the shores of Alaska in search of sea otter pelts. In the end, their ambitions collided with the ancestral claims of Native Americans, and a relationship that typically began with gift giving and tokens of respect corroded into bitterness and betrayal.

Despite the implied threat of Columbus's cannon fire, Guacanagari proceeded on the assumption that he and the white cacique were bound in good faith. They were a strange pair, the local chief who would prove indispensable to the visitors yet remain largely anonymous to history, and the tall, gray-haired adventurer from Genoa who would win lasting renown for an errant mission that had carried him westward in search of the Indies. Since first making landfall in the Caribbean two months earlier, Columbus had looked in vain for signs that he was at the threshold of the opulent Eastern realms of China and Japan. On Hispaniola, as elsewhere, Columbus found not golden-roofed temples and lords in sumptuous brocaded coats but simple huts and barely clad inhabitants. Still, he kept snatching at straws. He insisted on calling the people he met Indians, and when some of them referred to menacing residents of other islands as *canibas* or *caribas*—cannibals—he thought they meant *Khan-ibas,* or soldiers of China's Great Khan.

If these people were not the Orientals he had been seeking, Columbus was nonetheless taken by their generosity and evident simplicity. "Of anything they have, if you ask them for it, they never say no," he wrote. "Rather they invite the person to share it, and show as much love as if they were giving their hearts; and whether the things be of value or of small price, at once they are content with whatever little thing of whatever kind may be given to them." To Europeans, this contentment with

A relic of the devastated Taino culture, the elegantly carved mahogany spatula above was used by the island Indians to induce vomiting as part of a religious purification ritual.

Resembling the hammocks in which the Taino Indians slept, this chair, made from a single highly polished piece of wood, was used as the ceremonial seat for a tribal chief or high priest.

seeming trinkets such as glass beads appeared childlike. But to the Indians, exotic beads—often used to decorate objects of ceremonial importance—had the same timeless allure that gold did for the Europeans. Lacking an understanding of Taino culture, Columbus surmised that the islanders had little sense of value or property. He once reported to King Ferdinand and Queen Isabella that when he issued a proclamation in Spanish claiming all the islands and their inhabitants for the Crown, "nobody objected." In fact, when it became clear to the islanders that the visitors disdained Taino rituals and regarded the land and the people as theirs for the taking, many of the Indians fought fiercely to defend their territory.

The seeds of conflict were sown on the night the *Santa Maria* foundered. Columbus interpreted the loss of the ship as a sign from God that he should establish a settlement on the coast. Following his meeting with Guacanagari, he ordered the construction of a small fort from the ship's timbers and gave this first Spanish foothold in the New World the name La Navidad to honor its Christmas origins. Then on January 4, 1493, having draped his own cape of fine wool around the shoulders of his ally Guacanagari and leaving 38 volunteers to defend the fort, Columbus sailed for home. Setting a dubious precedent for future visitors to the New World, he took away a half-dozen Taino Indians to be displayed before the king and queen and to be instructed in Spanish so that they might serve as interpreters on future expeditions.

While he was gone, the Spaniards at La Navidad fell to quarreling among themselves and goaded the Taino by taking their women as concubines. When Columbus returned nearly a year later with a colonizing expedition of 17 ships and some 1,500 men, he found that the fort had been burned to the ground and the settlers killed. Speaking through a Taino interpreter, Guacanagari blamed the attack on a neighboring cacique and pointed to a bandage on his leg as proof that he had put up resistance. A Spanish physician examined him and found no wound beneath the dressing. But Columbus, mindful of the need for provisions as the colony established itself, chose to accept Guacanagari's story.

All the same, the era of amicable give-and-take between the Taino and the visitors

A beaded statuette with a mask on one side (right) and a face on the other, carved of rhinoceros horn imported from Africa by the Spaniards, represents a Taino zemi, or deity. Foremost among the zemis was a god of virgin birth who was both lord of the sea and giver of cassava, staple of the West Indian diet.

had ended. Forsaking the niceties of their first visit, Columbus and his men increasingly relied on force or the threat of it to extract gold and other resources from occupants of the interior. Guacanagari, hoping to improve his standing relative to rival chiefs, gave Columbus spies and warriors to deal with those Indians who defied the Spaniards and their guns. In the one-sided skirmishes that ensued, many hostile Taino were killed or captured.

Columbus eventually found a way of profiting from the prisoners. In 1496 he shipped nearly 500 of them to Spain; the 300 who survived the trip were sold on the block in Seville.

Meanwhile, the Spaniards had imposed another kind of servitude on the islanders. Every three months, Taino living in or near the new mining areas established in the interior were forced to pay a tribute of gold dust—enough to fill a cascabel, or hawk's bell. Indians elsewhere were each required to pay a quarterly levy of 25 pounds of cotton. Meeting these demands diverted effort from the cultivation of food at a time when the labor supply was being reduced by European-borne diseases, and a severe famine resulted. Such was the ill will between the Spaniards and the Indians that many colonists believed the fields were being deliberately neglected. One Spanish account estimated that 50,000 Indians died in the famine and claimed that "this calamity was the consequence of their own folly; for when they saw that the Spaniards wished to settle on their island, they thought they might expel them by creating a scarcity of food."

By 1500 the pressures of continuing food shortages, battles with surviving Indians, and disputes among the colonists themselves had eroded Columbus's authority, and he was ordered back to Spain. But the effort to squeeze further profit from Taino society continued.

Columbus's successor instituted the infamous encomienda system, which granted armed Spanish colonists title to large tracts of land or whole villages, along with sweeping authority over the Indians who lived there. In return for the labor they received, colonists were supposed to pay, protect, and Christianize their wards, officially known as "free vassals of the Crown." In practice, most Indians were treated as slaves, inciting protests from Roman Catholic missionaries, who tried to temper the abuses of the colonial system—one church-sponsored edict prohibited calling Indians dogs—but whose efforts left intact the basic framework of exploitation. The lords of Hispaniola simply replaced the encomienda with a new form of tribute requiring each cacique to provide a quantity of goods or a quota of workers.

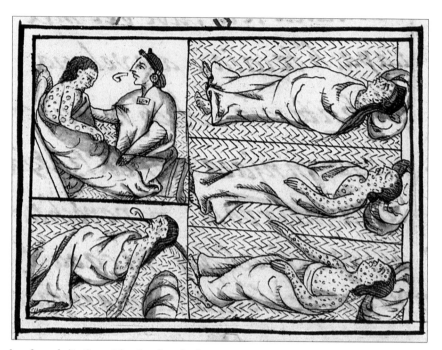

A doleful illustration found in an early history of New Spain pictures dying Indians covered with smallpox sores. This disease, along with common European childhood illnesses against which the Indians had no immunity, ravaged the native populations. "There was so much sickness and pestilence among them in all the land," a Spanish missionary reported, "that in most provinces more than half the people died."

By whatever name, Spanish policies tore at the roots of Taino culture. Entire villages were relocated to be nearer mines and farms. Caciques—who had traditionally claimed tribute from their subjects in return for protecting them in times of danger or want—became mere accessories in a campaign to extract labor and food from the burdened populace. Symptomatic of the Taino's demoralization was the fact that some women began bleaching their skin to make themselves more attractive to the invaders. But not even those Indians who sought to emulate the colonists could be sure of lasting rewards. After a decade of loyal service to the invaders, Guacanagari himself was turned upon by the Spaniards and died while trying to escape to the interior.

The final blow to the Taino was delivered by disease. In the New World, tribes living in relative isolation built up immunity to a small complement of indigenous diseases. The ports of the Old World, however, were clearinghouses for a host of exotic bacteria and viruses that originated in the far corners of Europe, Asia, and Africa and were spread by roving merchants and pilgrims. Thus, the Spanish colonists—who were immune to many of the Old World strains—exposed the Taino to virulent new diseases. Ever since Columbus landed on Hispaniola, measles, influenza, and other ills had been taking their toll. Then, in 1518, the first deadly plague of smallpox swept the island and spread to Puerto Rico, Cuba, and other Spanish outposts. One result of this epidemic was to spur the importation of African slaves to replace vanishing Indian labor.

No one knows how many people were living on Hispaniola when Columbus arrived there in 1492. According to conservative estimates, the population exceeded 100,000. By 1520 only 1,000 or so Indians remained. Within a single generation, a culture that had flourished on the island for more than a millennium had been destroyed, body and soul.

The tragedy of the Taino was not unique. Wherever the Spaniards found rich deposits of gold or silver—in the Caribbean, Mexico, or Peru—they instituted similar policies that together with the ravages of disease extinguished some Indian cultures and devastated others. At the same time, Spanish explorers were turning their attention to the uncharted shores of North America, probing the Atlantic and Gulf coasts in search of fresh mineral wealth. As it turned out, they would find little to extract there, but the few expeditions they carried out were enough to trigger wrenching changes in the life of the tribes they encountered. Chiefs hoping to appease the Spaniards would turn on their counterparts, epidemics would spread from village to village, and the bewildered survivors would abandon their haunted fields and hearths in search of a new place to live.

Unfortunately for the Indians spared these initial shocks, the lure of precious minerals was just the first of many incentives that drew ambitious Europeans of various nationalities to North America. Although gold proved scarce, other inducements beckoned—fertile land to be colonized and cultivated, sleek pelts and other prizes to be acquired in trade, and countless indigenous peoples to be converted to Christianity. Underlying these various motives was a fierce rivalry among the European powers for control of the assets of the New World.

In dealing with these intrusions, Native Americans labored under severe disadvantages. Aside from their susceptibility to disease, they were divided into myriad factions. At the time of Columbus, hundreds of distinct peoples inhabited North America, and many were made up of numerous chiefdoms—a multiplicity that abetted European efforts to play one party off against another. Furthermore, even the more aggressive tribes tended to regard warfare as an honorific ritual and were ill prepared to deal with relentless European tactics and weaponry.

Despite these weighty handicaps, Indians found ways of coping. War-

Discovered on Marco Island off Florida's west coast, this sleek panther carved of wood probably represented a deity of the Calusa, the tribe encountered by Ponce de León when he claimed Florida for Spain.

riors learned to avoid frontal assaults and harry the intruders to distraction; traders discovered that the Europeans too had their tribal disputes and managed to exploit them; shrewd chiefs forged coalitions and fended off white encroachments through diplomacy or intimidation. Few of these tactics succeeded for long, and for most native peoples, the European challenge proved to be a harrowing ordeal. But those who endured the trial bequeathed to their descendants the strength to remain faithful to their heritage through centuries of displacement and disparagement.

Even before the mineral wealth of Hispaniola and other Caribbean islands was depleted, Spanish conquistadors set out in search of new lands. In 1513 Juan Ponce de León, a veteran of Columbus's second voyage and a former governor of Puerto Rico, sailed northwestward to look for the land the Taino called Bimini. Although legend would romanticize his expedition as a quest for a fabled fountain of youth, he was driven by the same hope of enrichment that enticed other conquistadors. Just before Easter, Ponce de León's party made landfall on what he took to be Bimini. Actually, this was not an island, but a peninsula of the North American continent. He claimed this new land for Spain, and because his discovery came during the religious feast of the flowers, or *flores*, he christened it Florida. The name soon came to stand for a huge area of Spanish claims coinciding with the southeastern quadrant of the present United States.

Florida was scarcely uninhabited wilderness—as Ponce de León could attest. Before landing, while scouting the coast, his ship had been pelted with arrows shot by Indians from their twin-hulled dugout canoes. These warriors were Calusa, who inhabited the southern half of the peninsula. They were one of dozens of tribes across the Southeast whose combined population numbered at least one million. Most lived in villages not unlike those of Hispaniola, ranging in size from a few hundred people to several thousand. Along the region's sandy coasts and swampy estuaries, settlements tended to be smaller, and people subsisted mainly by fishing, gathering, and hunting, sometimes venturing from their home base for weeks or months on end in search of food. Farther inland, along the fertile banks of rivers and streams, villages were bigger, and the inhabitants were largely sedentary, depending as they did to a great extent on the cultivation of crops—especially that mainstay of the New World granary, corn.

Throughout the Southeast, villages were governed by chiefs and their relatives and retainers, who enjoyed special powers and privileges. These local chiefs, in turn, were subject to a paramount whose domain typically encompassed several villages. The great paramounts of the cultivated interior, however, might collect tribute from dozens of villages in the form of crops, raw materials, and labor— some of which went toward building and maintaining lavish ceremonial complexes, surrounded by stout palisades and dominated by massive earthen mounds that housed the remains of the distinguished dead. Within this system, power relationships were constantly being redefined. Periodically, a paramount might attempt to add new villages to his domain by force of arms, or an ambitious local chief might defy his overlord and seek tribute of his own. As a result, warfare was common, but its purpose was to intimidate opponents into compliance rather than annihilate them.

The determined hostility of the Calusa toward Ponce de León probably reflected something more than an innate wariness bred by local conflicts. The Calusa may have had previous contact with unauthorized raiding parties that ventured from the Caribbean in search of slaves. Certainly, the Calusa would have learned of the Spaniards—and of the misfortunes and diseases attending them—from Indians on nearby Cuba, which they visited in their big canoes for the purpose of trade.

Found in Calusa territory, this marvelously fierce rendition of a wolf's head—complete with menacing fangs and exaggerated ears—may have been incorporated into a shrine.

In the end, their antagonism proved to be more than the conquistador bargained for. After his pioneering foray, Ponce de León returned to the southwest coast of the Florida peninsula in 1521 with 200 men, livestock, and seeds, intent on founding a colony. He also brought with him Catholic priests and a new Crown policy known as the *Requerimiento,* or Notification. This proclamation, which was to be read in Spanish to the Indians, required the unwitting listeners to become subjects of Spain and convert to Christianity on the spot—or suffer death or enslavement. On this occasion, however, there was little time for such preliminaries. No sooner had Ponce de León led his settlers ashore than a vigilant band of Calusa unleashed their arrows, repelling the colonists and wounding their leader, who died after returning to Cuba.

Those who followed in his path fared little better in the face of unflagging resistance. By and large, the Spaniards reaped few rewards from their early ventures to Florida, but they did learn more about the Indians. One ill-fated yet revealing mission was launched in 1528 by Pánfilo de Narváez, an inept conquistador who landed near Tampa Bay in April with 400 men in search of a rich site to colonize. Marching northward, they provoked the Indians—first the Timucua and then the Apalachee around modern-day Tallahassee—by seizing hostages and stealing corn at every turn. In May they came upon one of the main Apalachee villages, and seeing only women and children there, took control without a fight.

Soon after the Spaniards marched in, the men of the village returned to find their settlement occupied. They tried to drive the well-armored intruders away with arrows, but were easily rebuffed, and came back

Timucua warriors armed with bows and spears emerge from their palisaded village to drive off raiders in an engraving made by Flemish printer Theodor de Bry from a drawing by the French artist-explorer Jacques le Moyne, whose original has since been lost. Other engravings based on le Moyne's portraits of Indian life in Florida, published by de Bry along with the artist's comments, appear on the following pages.

Three Timucuas disguised in deer hides and carrying bows and arrows ambush several deer at the edge of a stream. The Indians, wrote le Moyne, put the deer heads "on their own heads, so that they can see out through the eyes as through a mask," then attack "when the animals come to drink."

peacefully a few hours later, gesturing for the release of their women and children. Narváez agreed, but insisted on holding the chief hostage, which only provoked the Apalachee into renewing their assault the next day. This time they were bolder and set fire to several thatch houses the Spaniards had commandeered. Narváez's men leveled their muskets and drove the assailants off, but the Spaniards remained trapped for weeks. When they finally exhausted their provisions and fled the village, they proved easy targets for Apalachee archers who had adapted to the threat of firearms and lurked behind trees and fallen timbers. "They drove their arrows with such effect that they wounded many men and horses," wrote Narváez's treasurer, Álvar Núñez Cabeza de Vaca. "There were those this day who swore that they had seen two red oaks, each the thickness of the lower part of the leg, pierced through from side to side by arrows; and this is not so much to be wondered at, considering the power and skill with which the Indians are able to project them."

Certain now that this hostile territory harbored no riches worth exploiting, the weary Spaniards made their way to the Gulf Coast far north of their starting point and built flatboats in the hope of venturing westward along the shoreline to the infant colony of New Spain in Mexico. Once embarked, they were scattered by storm waves and wracked by hunger and thirst. In November

A group of young Timucua Indian men run, practice archery, and play a ball game. The object of the game, as explained by artist Jacques le Moyne, was to hit the wicker frame atop the pole with the ball: "He who strikes it first gets a prize."

A dramatic engraving shows the Timucua attacking a pair of alligators by shoving what le Moyne described as the "stem of a tree" into the mouths of the creatures, then flipping them onto their backs before killing them with arrows and clubs.

In another engraving derived from the work of Jacques le Moyne, Indians preserve fish and a wide variety of game, including several reptiles, by smoking the animals on a grate fashioned from green wood.

Cabeza de Vaca's boat capsized off an island along the present-day Louisiana or Texas coast, where he and his surviving companions were apprehended by Indians.

Although his men feared that they would be killed, Cabeza de Vaca had little choice but to put his party at the mercy of the Indians, who picked up the naked Spaniards bodily and carried them off to their homes, some distance away. "Because of the extreme coldness of the weather," he recalled, "they caused four or five very large fires to be placed at intervals, and at each they warmed us; and when they saw that we had regained some heat and strength, they took us to the next so swiftly that they hardly let us touch our feet to the ground. In this manner we went as far as their habitations, where we found that they had made a house for us with many fires in it." Baffled by such attentions, Cabeza de Vaca suspected that he and his men were being kept alive only to be sacrificed: "An hour after our arrival, they began to dance and hold great rejoicing, which lasted all night, although for us there was no joy, festivity, nor sleep, awaiting the hour they should make us victims." But the fears of the castaways were misplaced, he conceded: "In the morning, they again gave us fish and roots, showing us such hospitality that we were reassured."

After this promising start, relations between the two parties deteriorated. On a remote part of the island, Indians came across the remains of

some other marooned Spaniards from the Narváez expedition, who after their death had been carved up and eaten by their starving comrades. Horrified, the Indians scolded the surviving castaways so fiercely that Cabeza de Vaca feared they might all be put to death as cannibals. Soon thereafter, the Indians fell prey to a plague that carried away nearly half their population. "They conceived that we had destroyed them," the Spaniard wrote, "and believing it firmly, they concerted among themselves to dispatch those of us who survived." But the Indian who was guarding Cabeza de Vaca thwarted the plan by convincing the others that if the white men truly held the power of life and death, they should have been able to keep their own comrades from perishing.

In the end, the Spaniards were forced upon pain of starvation to put what magic they possessed at the disposal of the Indians by acting as

Shooting arrows tipped with flaming moss, the Timucua exact revenge on an enemy town by setting fire to the dry palm-branch roofs. Artist le Moyne noted that the warriors sometimes launched these attacks "by night in the utmost silence" and then made off swiftly once the roofs were ablaze.

healers. Local medicine men dispelled evil spirits by laying hands on the sick and blowing on the afflicted area. To avoid sacrilege, Cabeza de Vaca and his comrades came up with a Christian version of this ritual that entailed breathing on the patient, reciting the Lord's Prayer and a Hail Mary, and making the sign of the cross. This seemed to soothe their patients, and the Spaniards were rewarded with food and hides.

Along with such services, the castaways were expected to perform menial tasks. "Besides much other labor," Cabeza de Vaca wrote, "I had to get out roots from below the water and from among the cane where they grew in the ground. From this employment I had my fingers so worn that did a straw but touch them they would bleed." The Spaniard saw this as servitude, and indeed, Indians of the region sometimes kept captives from other tribes as slaves. As hard as their lot was, though, the men stranded on the island fared little worse than the people they served, who often had to scrounge for subsistence.

Cabeza de Vaca eventually gained some freedom of movement by acting as a trader. "The Indians would beg me to go from one quarter to another for things of which they have need," he recalled, "for in consequence of incessant hostilities, they cannot traverse the country, nor make many exchanges." As a neutral, he was able to pass safely between the coast and the interior, carrying pearls and shells from the island and bringing back skins, ocher for body paint, and cane and sinews for crafting bows and arrows. After several years of this existence, Cabeza de Vaca profited by his knowledge of the country and its people to make his way westward with three other surviving members of the expedition. They wandered toward Mexico, plying their skills as healers along the way and acquiring an admiring train of Indians, until at last they reached New Spain, six years after their grueling odyssey began.

Although the tale told by Cabeza de Vaca and his companions offered scant encouragement to those seeking fortune in Florida, hopes persisted. Some thought that exploration of the interior might yet reveal mineral wealth like that found in New Spain. At the very least, the Spaniards wanted to establish an overland route from Mexico to the Atlantic Coast that would enable their galleons to avoid the shoals and storms that often claimed ships in the Gulf. These incentives were enough to enlist the efforts of one of the most accomplished Spanish conquistadors, Hernando de Soto, who had aided Francisco Pizarro mightily in the subjection and looting of the Inca Empire of Peru from 1531 to 1535. Now, nearing the age of 40, de Soto was ready to stake his wealth and reputation on the boldest attempt yet to exploit Florida. In 1539 he mustered an expedition of nine ships and 600 soldiers, accompanied by assorted tailors, blacksmiths, priests, slaves, and at least two female servants, along with more than 200 cavalry horses and a herd of 300 pigs for meat on the hoof.

In late May, the ships sailed into Tampa Bay, not far from the Gulf Coast landfall of the ill-fated Narváez. This was the northern fringe of hostile Calusa territory, but de Soto's scouts found friendlier Timucua Indians inland—and claimed an unexpected prize in the person of Juan Ortiz, a survivor of the Narváez fiasco whose arms had been tattooed Indian-style and whose naked body was so sunburned that he was scarcely distinguishable from his hosts. Ortiz had found asylum with the Timucua after escaping from the Calusa, who had enslaved him. He had since mastered the native language, and he became de Soto's interpreter and intermediary with the various Indians they encountered. As they marched into the interior, Ortiz would be the last link in a human translation chain that sometimes included three or four Indians, each of whom would translate into his own tongue until the language was Timucuan, which Ortiz then could convert into Spanish.

After spending about six weeks near the coast gathering intelligence and girding for the long trek, de Soto broke camp and marched north. He and his troops cut a brutal swath, paying little heed to the dozen priests accompanying them or to a royal decree from King Charles V ordering them to pacify the region without "death and robbery of the Indians." They came across numerous villages, which usually consisted of 20 to 30 mud-plastered wood huts housing about 10 persons each and arranged around a central plaza. Each village typically had a chief who watched over storehouses of corn, dried meat, and other goods.

De Soto made use of both the storehouses and the chiefs. In a tactic first employed by Spaniards to drive the Moors from Spain the previous century, he routinely kidnapped local chiefs. He then held them hostage for food and for slaves—Indian men to carry supplies, women to serve as concubines. Male slaves were usually shackled in iron collars and chains. Anyone who attempted to escape or otherwise contrived to displease him was thrown to the dogs—mastiffs and wolfhounds bred to tear their victims to pieces. "This governor," wrote de Soto's secretary, "was much given to the sport of slaying Indians."

European technology further stacked the odds in de Soto's favor. In addition to smoothbore muskets and crossbows, his men were equipped with protective plate and chain mail, swords, lances, and halberds—

spiked battle-axes mounted on long poles. Their Indian opponents knew the territory intimately, of course, and were often effective attacking from ambush with their bows, clubs, and spears. But the invaders' horses gave them an edge even when surrounded. This was fearsomely illustrated in mid-September in Florida's northern panhandle at a village called Napituca. When hundreds of Indians encircled de Soto in an attempt to recover one of their kidnapped chiefs, he ordered a charge by his cavalry. His lancers, numbering perhaps 100 mounted men, skewered and killed as many as 300 Indians and captured hundreds more.

After wintering in the Apalachee town of Anhaica, where the occupiers were harassed by the same kind of hit-and-run attacks that had bedeviled Narváez, the Spaniards resumed their search for riches in March 1540, moving northward in an unwieldy procession whose ranks swelled to nearly 1,000 people with the addition of captured Indians. Their goal was a village that an Apalachee hostage had described to interpreter Ortiz in lavish terms. Called Cofitachequi, it was said to be governed by a lovely Indian princess and possessed of much gold. People along de Soto's traumatic trail were learning to rid themselves of the Spaniards by telling them of riches that lay just beyond.

In search of Cofitachequi, the expedition passed through the heart of present-day Georgia, where the Spaniards encountered villages with both summer and winter houses—a common custom among Indians of the interior Southeast, with its seasonal extremes. "Each of the Indians has his house for the winter plastered inside and out," reported a member of the expedition who called himself the Gentleman of Elvas. "They shut the very small door at night and build a fire inside so that it

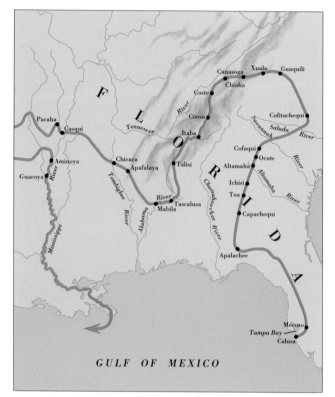

The route of de Soto's expedition through the American South to the Mississippi and beyond is shown below, along with the names of the Indian tribes he encountered.

Evidence of another of Hernando de Soto's camps, glass beads made in Spain during the 16th century were found north of modern-day Tampa.

Left behind by de Soto's expedition, a brass bell meant as a gift for the Indians was discovered not far from the Spaniards' 1539-1540 winter camp near Tallahassee.

This early-1500s Spanish copper coin, found in Florida on de Soto's route, was minted specifically for use in the New World.

gets as hot as an oven, and stays so all night long so there is no need of clothing. Besides those houses, they have others for summer, with kitchens nearby where they build their fires and bake their bread.'' The same witness noted that the houses of the chiefs were larger than the rest and surrounded by sheds "in which they gather together the tribute paid them by their Indians, which consists of maize and deerskins and native blankets resembling shawls.''

Pushing on in search of greater wealth, the Spaniards reached what is now South Carolina and came upon a river, across which lay the sought-after settlement of Cofitachequi. At first blush, it appeared to live up to its reputation. De Soto was met there as promised by a handsome young woman, who was carried to the water on a litter by Indian bearers and ferried across in a large, ornate canoe. One Spaniard likened her to Cleopatra—"brown but well proportioned.'' De Soto's secretary wrote that she "spoke to the governor quite gracefully and at her ease. She was a young girl of fine bearing; and she took off a string of pearls that she wore on her neck and put it on the governor as a necklace to show her favor and to gain his goodwill.''

This regal figure, whom the Spaniards called the "cacica,'' was in fact the niece of the province's female chief—one of two then known in all of Florida. She may have been her aunt's legitimate heir, but she had no gold to offer. Freshwater pearls were the village's only precious commodity. The Spaniards proceeded to plunder burial places of some 200 pounds of the pearls, left as offerings to the dead.

An iron horseshoe, unearthed at the site of an Indian village in Alabama, may be a relic of either de Soto's expedition or of another foray led by Tristán de Luna y Arellano 20 years later.

At the cacica's invitation, de Soto and company then visited the nearby village of Talimeco, an important ceremonial center crowned by an imposing mortuary temple some 100 feet long and 40 feet wide, erected atop an immense pile of earth. This platform mound, shaped like a truncated pyramid, was emblematic of a centuries-old tradition known to posterity as the Mississippian culture because it evolved along that river before spreading to other fertile areas of the Southeast. Inside the high temple stood lifelike wooden statues of men and women, some of them holding axes and other weapons, as if guarding the remains of the revered dead deposited there. Undeterred, the Spaniards carried away a trunkful of pearls from the sanctuary.

As de Soto and his men discovered, death had been a frequent visitor

to Talimeco and environs. Many hamlets had been transformed into ghost towns by recent epidemics—triggered, perhaps, by an abortive Spanish effort to colonize the South Carolina coast 15 years earlier.

When de Soto was ready to move on, he followed his harsh precedent by taking the cacica hostage and bringing her along, retainers and all—an act that even his follower the Gentleman of Elvas denounced as a poor return "for the goodwill she had shown him." She refused to be kept for long, however. Several days later, she left the trail the expedition was following, taking with her a coffer of pearls, and walked into the woods, explaining to her escorts that she had to "attend to her necessities." It was the last de Soto saw of her.

Hoping to find his fortune in the highlands as he had in Peru, de Soto struck out next toward the northwest, crossing the mountain chain known today as the Blue Ridge and reaching present-day Tennessee. When this grueling foray proved fruitless, he cut back to the southwest and entered the province of Coosa, a fertile Mississippian stronghold whose paramount held sway over numerous settlements and received word of de Soto's approach from messengers well in advance. When the

A prominent member of the expedition—perhaps de Soto himself—severs the foot of an Indian victim in a late-16th-century engraving that purports to illustrate the dreadful tortures inflicted on the native peoples by the Spaniards as they marched through Florida, Georgia, and Alabama in search of the Indians' supposed hoards of gold.

*Sign of Spanish bru-
tality, the skull of a
Coosa Indian shows
a fatal wound above
the right eye that,
from its size and
shape, was doubt-
less inflicted by a
Spanish sword. This
skull of an older
male was found
amid those of other
victims, including
many women.*

Spaniards reached his main village in mid-July, the paramount received them royally with serenading flute players and singers, then escorted them into the town and lodged them in houses that his subjects had been ordered to vacate for the purpose. Such hospitality was a time-honored form of diplomacy among peoples of the New World—a way of averting conflict by instilling in the honored guest a reciprocal obligation of courtesy. Yet de Soto had repeatedly defied the customs of the country, and this was no exception. He placed the paramount under armed guard, causing the villagers to flee to the woods, where most were later rounded up, chained, and added to the legion of slaves.

De Soto evidently believed he could go on committing such betrayals without the Indians growing any the wiser. But he had entered a well-settled land with effective lines of communication, and as he moved south, his reputation preceded him.

Gaining the upper reaches of the Alabama River in early October, he came upon the main village of a populous chiefdom called Tascalusa, ruled by a shrewd paramount of the same name. This stern figure awaited de Soto atop a mound in the central square. Shielded by a deerskin sunshade held by a retainer, and wearing a feathered cape and high headdress, he remained seated "in perfect composure as if he had been a king," the Gentleman of Elvas noted, while dancers performed in honor of the visitors.

When de Soto subsequently seized Tascalusa and demanded 400 men and 100 women to replace Indian bearers and concubines who had died or escaped en route, the paramount gave him the men but informed him that he would have to wait until they reached one of his tributary villages, Mabila, to get the women. Anticipating ill-treatment, Tascalusa may already have prepared that fortified village as a trap; if not, his messengers now made sure that Mabila was ready to receive the Spaniards.

De Soto entered Mabila on October 18 with his hostage Tascalusa and a small advance guard, carrying the expedition's valuables. Once they were inside the log palisade girding the village, Tascalusa withdrew from the Spaniards and entered one of many houses where his warriors were waiting with bows and arrows. When de Soto tried to coax him out, the Indians burst from their shelters, killing several Spaniards and forcing de Soto and the rest back through the gates. De Soto promptly drew up his main force, with mounted lancers in the fore, and stormed the village, putting it to the torch. One witness claimed that women and boys joined in the defense of Mabila, and that some threw themselves into the fire rather than be enslaved. An estimated 3,000 warriors and villagers died. Tascalusa reportedly escaped before the counterattack, but his chiefdom would never be the same.

The battle of Mabila also cost de Soto dearly. The Spaniards lost not only 22 dead and 150 wounded but also the valuables the advance guard had left behind—including looted pearls, clothing, and sacramental wine. In the bitter aftermath, one chronicler noted, de Soto's followers began to suspect "that it was impossible to dominate such bellicose people or to subjugate men who were so free."

True to form, de Soto rejected the prudent option of marching to the Gulf of Mexico, where ships waited to resupply or evacuate his weary party. Instead, he set up winter camp along Tibbee Creek in present-day Mississippi, then continued on to the north and west in the spring, blown hither and yon by the latest rumor of riches. Although some Indians staged night raids on the Spaniards, many chiefs concluded that resistance was futile and sought to appease the intruders. Reaching the province of Casqui, near present-day Memphis, de Soto was met by a cacique who addressed him as "the son of the sun"—the highest form of praise in the Mississippian culture, whose leaders claimed descent from the sun god. When the cacique asked him for a sign of his power, de Soto had his men erect a large cross on a hill, knowing that the Indians considered mounds to be sacred. The Spaniards then approached on bended knees to kiss the cross, and the Indians followed suit, after which they built a cane fence around the cross to enclose it as they did their own holy places. A short time later, much-needed rain fell, and the cacique took it as confirmation that the cross brought blessings. He placed his men at de Soto's disposal, and together they overran a rival province nearby.

Other chiefs tried to achieve a kind of kinship with de Soto by giving him their daughters, sisters, or wives—an accepted form of alliance building among the Indians but an embarrassment to de Soto's secretary, who knew that his commander had a wife in Spain. He worried that the polygamous chiefs would conclude that Christian lords too "could have as many wives and concubines as they desired." De Soto himself evidently

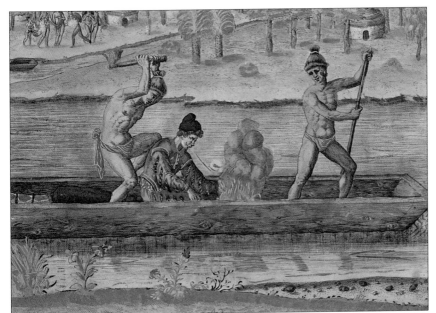

A Florida Indian standing in a canoe prepares to split the skull of his unsuspecting French passenger in a de Bry engraving based on a picture by le Moyne, who observed Indians in the vicinity of the ill-fated French colony of Fort Caroline and was one of the few to escape when Spanish forces overran that stronghold in 1565.

had no such scruples about accepting the women, nor did he feel obligated to those who offered them.

Having flouted virtually every code the Indians lived by with seeming impunity, de Soto finally fell prey to despondency and some sort of fever, perhaps malaria, the following spring. He died near the Mississippi River on May 21, 1542, surrounded by a dwindling host of followers. His lieutenant, Luis de Moscoso, took command, hoping not for gold or conquest but mere survival. He tried reaching Mexico overland through Texas, but the seminomadic Indians there lacked enough stored food for the Spaniards to live on. Retracing their steps to the Mississippi, they built barges and started downstream, harried much of the way by warriors in dugouts carrying up to 50 men.

The 300 or so Spanish survivors who finally found safe harbor on the Mexican coast in September 1543 had little to show for their efforts, other than the 100 Indian slaves who accompanied them. Yet the impact of their venture on the region had been enormous. Through enslavement, looting, and conquest, the Spaniards had disrupted food production and other elements of the native economy. By repeatedly humiliating chiefs and violating grave sites and other sanctuaries, de Soto had undermined the spiritual foundations of the culture. And even those depredations were dwarfed by the lethal consequences of the diseases his men had communicated. Epidemics raged from village to village, killing untold thousands and bringing many chiefdoms to the brink of collapse.

Evidence of this abrupt decline was provided by another Spanish expedition less than two decades later. In 1559 a single detachment from an abortive colonizing effort led by Tristán de Luna y Arellano—whose ships and supplies had been ravaged by a hurricane shortly after they put in at Pensacola Bay—ventured north through territory explored earlier by de Soto. Some members of this detachment had marched with de Soto, and they were amazed by the changes they witnessed. Much of the chiefdom of the defiant Tascalusa was now sparsely populated or abandoned. Far-

ther north in once-thriving Coosa, villages had declined in number and size, leaving few people to produce food for the chief and his retinue or construct
platform mounds. Groups that had paid tribute to the
paramount of Coosa were now in rebellion. The land
"looked so much the worse to the Spaniards for having been depicted so grandly," the expedition's chronicler wrote. Veterans of de Soto's march wondered
sadly if they had been bewitched when they witnessed
Coosa before in its glory.

The dismal results of these early expeditions to
Florida had all but extinguished Spanish interest in the
region when the appearance of foreign rivals rekin-
dled the flame. In 1564 French Huguenots—Protestant
reformers detested by the Spanish Catholics—founded
the colony of Fort Caroline at the mouth of the Saint
Johns River, a location that offered a base for French
privateers preying on Spanish treasure ships in the Atlantic. The settlers soon faced privation and had to either steal food from the local Timucua or trade with
them on unfavorable terms; Frenchmen complained of
giving up "the very shirts from their backs to get one
fish." The Spaniards responded to the French intrusion by dispatching an expedition of 800 soldiers and
colonists under Pedro Menéndez de Avilés, commander of the West Indies Fleet. Menéndez de Avilés
landed south of Fort Caroline in 1565, and guided by
Indians hostile to the French, launched a surprise assault overland while the outpost's defenders were expecting an attack from the sea. His men overwhelmed
the fort, then tracked down most of the Huguenots
who had fled the stockade and slaughtered them.

Having ruthlessly fulfilled the first part of his orders, Menéndez de
Avilés proceeded to the second part: establishing a permanent Spanish
presence in Florida. The first settlement, Saint Augustine, was founded at
the point 40 miles south of Fort Caroline where Menéndez de Avilés had
landed on Saint Augustine's feast day; a second, Santa Elena, was planted at the mouth of Port Royal Sound on the South Carolina coast.

To the surrounding Indians, these outposts were highly provocative.

*Cannon and heavy muskets known as har-
quebuses poke menacingly through
gunports in a 16th-century watercolor offering a bird's-eye view of the Spanish fort at
Saint Augustine. Founded in 1565 by Pedro
Menéndez de Avilés, Saint Augustine
became the capital of the colony of Florida
and was subject to attacks not only by Indians but also by hostile English forces.*

Horned devils exult as they carry off a naked Indian in a woodcut used by Spanish missionaries to frighten the native peoples into converting to Christianity. By the 1700s, the priests had founded more than 100 missions across Florida.

Local caciques resented the claims of the intruders, and villagers were prey to unruly soldiers from the Spanish garrisons who pillaged houses and sometimes abducted the women. When Indians struck back, the soldiers launched punitive expeditions against them, and hostilities escalated.

A different sort of challenge to the indigenous peoples came from Catholic missions that soon sprang up along the Atlantic and Gulf coasts. Typically, a priest or two would prevail on a village chief to tolerate their presence if not to embrace their God; they would then build a church in or near the village and try to win converts. Although the main objective of the missions was to save souls, they also served the interests of the colony by keeping Indians under control. In consultation with civil authorities, priests used their influence with the Indians to arrange unions between high-ranking native women and Spanish soldiers or dignitaries, thus increasing Spanish influence within the tribe. Governor Menéndez de Avilés himself, although he already had a wife back home, wed the sister of the Calusa paramount in a ceremony missionaries reluctantly agreed to in order to improve relations with that previously hostile group. A lesser Spanish official took as his wife the chief of a Timucua village near Saint Augustine, who accepted Catholicism herself and then helped convert her subjects. Later, the colonists installed her as chief of a mission along the Georgia coast.

The missions also served as conduits for a system of tribute like that introduced on Hispaniola. At first, Indian chiefs had to forward through the missions an annual levy of corn, hides, and other commodities. Later, they had to send quotas of men to Saint Augustine to build fortifications and perform other labors. In mission villages, Indians maintained separate fields to support the church. The priests, for their part, brought in many Old World foods—including peas, garlic, and oranges—and introduced metal hoes to speed production.

The mission system worked best with sedentary societies like the Apalachee. Seminomadic groups that still depended on foraging for subsistence seldom stood still long enough to be evangelized. A Spaniard complained that the Guale of the Georgia and South Carolina coast were "scattered about the country for nine of the 12 months of the year, so that to influence them at all, one missionary was needed for each Indian." For every village that embraced the priests, there were many others that resisted. The Guale might have been more accepting if they had been asked simply to add Christian rites to their existing ones. But they balked when the men in robes insisted that theirs was the only way. Indian hostility forced one order of missionaries, the Jesuits, to give up their campaign and go home. Resistance to the missions among the Guale led to such fierce attacks at Santa Elena that the outpost was abandoned in 1586.

A particular bone of contention was the priests' opposition to polygamy, a practice that was not limited to chiefs. Among some local tribes, men commonly cohabited with their wives' sisters. In 1597 a Franciscan friar denounced a Christianized Guale named Don Juanillo for taking more than one wife—a sin that the church had earlier indulged in the case of Governor Menéndez de Avilés. To make matters worse, the friar tried to deprive the Indian of his right to a tribal leadership position. "They take away our women," Don Juanillo angrily told his people, "leaving us only the one and perpetual, forbidding us to exchange her." The incident, capping nearly three decades of church interference in Guale traditions, touched off a rampage. Warriors raided missions that had held out along the coast after Santa Elena was abandoned, burning at least one church, and murdering five missionaries. They beat and then humiliated the one surviving Franciscan by making him clean a Guale burial temple—"the house of the demon," he called it—and then stand in a cornfield and pose as a scarecrow.

The uprising did not deflect the mission builders for long. Within a half-century of Saint Augustine's founding, Spanish Florida contained at least 50 missions that exercised control over more than 25,000 Indians. While spreading Catholicism, these outposts also transmitted European diseases. Even before the missionaries arrived, Florida had suffered several major epidemics, including bubonic plague and smallpox. The missions, where Europeans came in daily contact with their vulnerable charges, compounded the devastation. In the end, the combined effect on the native peoples of disease, demoralization, and economic disruption was nothing short of apocalyptic. By the mid-18th century, only a few hundred Indians remained on the entire Florida peninsula.

Two decades after the Spaniards ousted the French from Florida, another European power appeared on the scene to stake its claim. In 1585 the English established a settlement on Roanoke Island, just inside the Outer Banks of present-day North Carolina. Like the French, the English had begun their New World expeditions far to the north, around Newfoundland, before being drawn southward by the desire to contend with Spain for control of territory and sea lanes. The main promoter of the privately financed Roanoke expedition was Sir Walter Raleigh, a favorite of Queen Elizabeth I, who forbade him to take part in the journey because she wanted him close to home. Raleigh in turn honored the Virgin Queen by bestowing on the northern tier of what the Spaniards called Florida a new title—Virginia. As the English defined it, this sprawling domain extended northward from the Outer Banks to French-claimed Canada and westward to the largely uncharted Pacific, which they hoped to reach by an inland waterway.

Like other Europeans who had designs on the New World, Raleigh and company were far more concerned with the maneuvers of their Old World rivals than with the prerogatives of the Indians. The real powers the Virginia colonists would have to reckon with, however, were not the Spaniards—whose warships would search in vain for the new English colony—but cunning Indian chiefs, whose authority would so impress the English that they would sometimes refer to them as kings. For their part, the tribes of the region—members of the vast Algonquian language family—called their leaders werowances, meaning men who are rich, or wise. The riches came from a tribute system similar to that practiced by the mound-building peoples of the Southeast. Villagers offered a portion of their goods—including corn, game, hides, and treasures such as pearls—to the village chief, who in turn passed on part of his yield to the werowance, or paramount. In exchange, the werowance was expected to act wisely, storing goods for the people in times of want and offering rewards to warriors, priests, and councilors who guarded his domain against physical or spiritual threats.

Unlike the Mississippian paramounts, the werowances of Virginia did not build vast ceremonial complexes. But they had few peers in North America when it came to bold leadership. Some of them installed their relatives as village chiefs to bolster their power. Through this and other forms of control, a shrewd overlord named Powhatan—a paramount among paramounts—was building an empire along Chesapeake Bay and its tributaries when the first settlers reached Roanoke Island. Although the new colony lay south of his emerging domain, Powhatan would cast a long shadow over English efforts in the decades to come.

The leaders of the Roanoke expedition knew almost nothing of the local inhabitants they would encounter, but they recognized the need to accommodate them. As Protestants, they professed horror at the behavior of the Catholic Spaniards toward the Indians and thought that they could do better; as pragmatists, they realized that they could ill afford to scare away people they would depend on for food and know-how.

The preliminaries were promising. When a two-ship scouting expedition reached Roanoke Island in advance of the main party, the English invited a curious Indian on board and presented him with a hat and a shirt, among other novelties. Not content with simply receiving gifts, the Indian paddled off in his canoe and returned a short time later with two loads of fish, one for each crew. Arthur Barlowe, captain of one of the vessels, remarked that such generosity was typical of the inhabitants, who called themselves the Roanoke. "We were entertained with all love, and kindness, and with as much bounty, after their manner, as they could possibly devise," he wrote. "We found the people most gentle, loving, and faithful, void of all guile and treason." The Indians were not so innocent as to give up their valuables without a fair return, however. They had already made contact with European privateers and knew what they wanted most from the white men—metal tools such as knives and hatchets that would ease their tasks.

The scouting party soon made the acquaintance of a prominent figure on Roanoke Island named Granganimeo, who received them on a long mat, at the far end of which sat four lesser dignitaries. Seeking to be diplomatic, the English offered gifts to the four as well as to their leader, but Granganimeo promptly took away their presents and placed them in

VIEWS OF
THE ALGONQUIANS

Among the most accurate of all early pictures of Indians are those made by the skilled English watercolorist John White, who accompanied the first English expedition to Roanoke Island in 1585. White's job was to make a visual record of everything that was discovered—or as official instructions to artists on such missions put it, to "draw to life one of each kind of thing that is strange to us in England," including "birds, beasts, fishes, herbs, trees, and fruits," along with "the figures and shapes of men and women."

White—who later returned as the leader of a second expedition to Roanoke Island—spent more than one year there and on the adjacent mainland during his initial stay. He explored tirelessly, making hundreds of field sketches of the Algonquian-speaking inhabitants, their villages, their occupations, and their dress. The artist was able to compile a visual representation of the Indians before European influences could affect their habits and ways of life. His finished pictures, such as that of a cooking grill below and the composite view of various Indian fishing techniques at right, offer an authentic view of these people as they had lived for hundreds of years prior to the arrival of the white man.

In White's composite, an Indian trolls with a dip net (right) from a dugout canoe, where a fire has been kindled to provide visibility at night, while in the background, fish are being speared or trapped in a weir (left).

In this view of a large Algonquian village called Secotan, drawn by White in 1585, some Indians perform a dance in a sacred circle of posts while others sit for a meal beside baskets of food. The houses, made of poles covered with reed matting, border a wide main street. Other features portrayed by White are a fire for prayers and fields of corn in three stages of growth, some ripening, some ready for harvest, some "newly sprong," as White notes. The hut in the top cornfield houses a boy assigned to serve as a scarecrow.

Their rype corne

Their greene corne.

Corne newly sprong.

Their sitting at meate

The place of solemne prayer.

The howse wherin the Tombe of their Herounds standeth

SECOTON.

A Ceremony in their prayers wth strange testius and songs dansing abowt posts carued on the topps lyke mens faces.

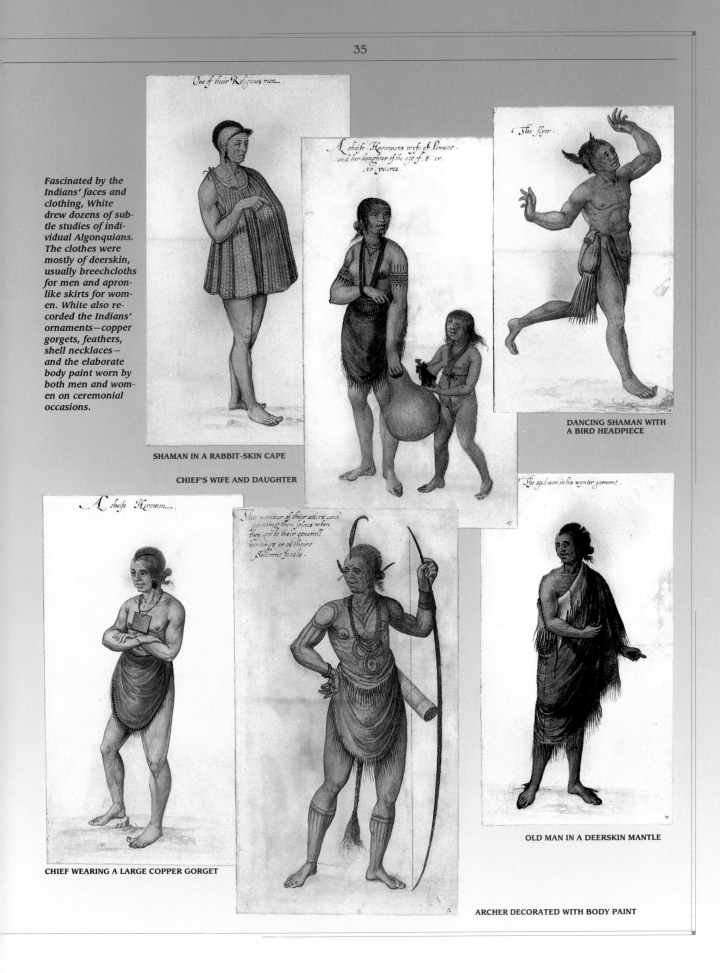

Fascinated by the Indians' faces and clothing, White drew dozens of subtle studies of individual Algonquians. The clothes were mostly of deerskin, usually breechcloths for men and apron-like skirts for women. White also recorded the Indians' ornaments—copper gorgets, feathers, shell necklaces—and the elaborate body paint worn by both men and women on ceremonial occasions.

SHAMAN IN A RABBIT-SKIN CAPE

CHIEF'S WIFE AND DAUGHTER

DANCING SHAMAN WITH A BIRD HEADPIECE

CHIEF WEARING A LARGE COPPER GORGET

OLD MAN IN A DEERSKIN MANTLE

ARCHER DECORATED WITH BODY PAINT

Another White drawing shows the bodies of 10 notables lying in the charnel house of the village of Secotan. The dead, watched over by a crouching effigy called a Kywash (right), were mummified by replacing their perishable innards with a padding of deerskin. Flesh removed from the dead was dried in the sun and packed in the bundles at their feet.

The Tombe of their Cherounes or cheife personages, their flesh clene taken of from the bones save the skynn and heare of theire heads, wch flesh is dried and enfolded in mats laide at theire feete. their bones also being made dry ar couered wth deare skynns not altering their forme or proportion. With theire Kywash, which is an Image of woode keeping the deade.

his own basket, thus making it clear to the visitors that all wealth on the island flowed through him. This was no idle boast. As the English discovered, Granganimeo was the brother of the Roanoke werowance, Wingina, and had been sent to the island to oversee activities there while Wingina recuperated from a battle wound at his base on the mainland. By paying court to Wingina's brother, the scouting party thus gained access to the ultimate authority in the area and advanced the cause of their colony. They were also helped by the fact that the Roanoke deemed the scraggly island of secondary importance. Their main villages were located on the mainland, where the soil was rich enough to support crops in abundance, and they used the island primarily as a campsite for fishing and foraging. Thus an English settlement there would be less of an intrusion.

The Roanoke proved to be good neighbors when the full-scale expedition arrived in the summer of 1585. Wingina allowed the 100 or so settlers, including a number of soldiers, to build a fort and cottages on the northern end of the 16-mile-long island. Not far away stood two Roanoke hamlets, or seasonal campsites, each consisting of perhaps a dozen long houses extending up to 30 feet and covered with woven mats affixed to wooden posts. From the start, the settlers were largely dependent on the Indians for sustenance because many of their provisions had been lost when one of their ships ran aground on treacherous shoals off the island. In exchange for tools and cloth, the Roanoke built weirs in which the newcomers could trap fish, and plied them with venison and vegetables. Besides their skill at hunting and fishing, the Indians were also gifted farmers, whose techniques included planting beans in the same hills as corn. The beans took support from the corn by growing up the stalks and returned nutrients through their roots to fertilize the corn. The Roanoke harvest of more than 100 bushels of corn per acre amazed the English.

Another New World crop, tobacco—first introduced in Europe a half-century earlier by Spanish conquistadors from the Caribbean—intrigued the settlers as well. The Indians considered the plant sacred and smoked its dried leaf ceremonially in clay pipes. Thomas Harriot, the colony's 25-year-old naturalist who studied the Roanoke closely and learned their language, thought tobacco was responsible for their general vigor. "It purgeth superfluous phlegm and other gross humors," he claimed, and "openeth all the pores and passages of the body." Notions such as these encouraged Europeans to make an everyday habit of a narcotic that the Indians reserved for special occasions. Harriot himself smoked tobacco so assiduously that he reportedly died of cancer.

The Roanoke were even more impressed with the wonders the Englishmen brought to the New World—not just the firearms but also Harriot's compasses and other instruments that appeared magical. Another quality that set the visitors apart in the eyes of the Indians was their remarkable abstinence: Harriot wrote that the Roanoke marveled "that we had no women amongst us, neither did we care for any of theirs." In fact, expedition leaders had vowed to execute anyone who provoked the Indians by assaulting their women. But the main reason the Englishmen were deemed otherworldly was their apparent immunity to influenza and other diseases inflicted on the Indians after the colony was established. Noticing that a village could be decimated by disease even if white men were not present, the Roanoke pleaded with them on one occasion to punish an enemy village with their "invisible bullets"—and thanked them profusely when disease struck. "Some people could not tell whether to think us gods or men," wrote Harriot.

As the months wore on, however, reverence for the settlers gave way

In an engraving of a John White watercolor entitled "The Arrival of the Englishmen in Virginia," a pinnace approaches Roanoke Island. Two larger English vessels stand off the dangerous Outer Banks, which have already claimed a number of wrecks.

This haunting, enigmatic mask of carved shell, which was discovered in Virginia, is similar to works of the ancient Mississippian Indians, an indication that the tribes dwelling in Virginia during Powhatan's era were influenced artistically by the distant mound-building civilization.

to contempt. By the spring of 1586, the English had grown so destitute and dependent that some Indians began to question the power of their God. To make matters worse, the settlers' ally Granganimeo died in April, leaving no buffer between them and Wingina, who appeared increasingly reluctant to support a colony that continued to rely on Indian provisions. Even for skilled farmers such as the Roanoke, spring was a lean time, and Wingina had to look to the needs of his own. The colony's governor, Colonel Ralph Lane, a hot-tempered veteran of the cruel English campaign to colonize Ireland, became convinced—with some reason, perhaps—that Wingina was no longer willing to tolerate the presence of hungry and potentially hostile settlers and was enlisting other tribes in a plot against them.

Lane made a plan to stifle the suspected conspiracy at its source. On June 1, 1586, he led a contingent of soldiers to Wingina's home. Lane entered the village on the pretense of meeting with the werowance, then shouted the signal for the attack: "Christ our Victory!"

At that, he opened fire with his pistol, wounding Wingina, who managed to struggle to his feet and flee into the woods, closely pursued by Lane's men. A short time later, one of them returned carrying Wingina's head.

Fearful of reprisals from the Roanoke and close to starvation, the colonists were reluctant to remain on the island. Deliverance came a week later, when Sir Francis Drake appeared with his fleet of English warships, fresh from a raid on the Spaniards at Saint Augustine. At the settlers' insistence, Drake carried home all but a few colonists, who were off on an expedition at the time and were never heard from again.

Lane's attack on Wingina had grave consequences for future attempts to colonize the area. A month after Drake sailed away, a task force carrying supplies and reinforcements for the original colony arrived to find the settlers gone. Fifteen men were left to hold the fort; they were

Enthroned on a platform in a long house and attended by his councilors and wives, the great Indian chief known as Powhatan appears much as he did to Captain John Smith in 1607, the year Smith helped found the English colony at Jamestown. The engraving illustrated a map of Virginia drawn by Captain John Smith, published in 1612.

later attacked by the Roanoke and their allies, who killed one Englishman and forced the rest out to sea, where they disappeared.

The following summer, a second major expedition arrived from England, this one made up of 110 people, including both men and women. The governor of the colony, John White—a veteran of the first expedition and a gifted artist who faithfully recorded many native customs—brought with him an Indian named Manteo, who had willingly accompanied the settlers back to England the year before. Manteo was a prominent member of the Croatoan tribe, which controlled the stretch of the Outer Banks just below Roanoke Island, and White hoped to use him to reach an accord with that tribe. Manteo's people duly welcomed the English, but mindful of recent events, they made it clear that they could offer the settlers no corn. Any lingering hopes that the colonists had of receiving such assistance were dashed a short time later when a party of English soldiers guided by Manteo, seeking revenge for the attack on their garrison the year before, entered a Roanoke village and killed or wounded a number of men, women, and children—only to discover too late that the town had been abandoned by the Roanoke and that the victims were friendly Croatoans out foraging.

Keenly aware of their isolation in the wake of this debacle, the colonists sent Governor White back to England with the supply ships to ensure that they would soon be reinforced and reprovisioned. But White's best efforts were stymied by the escalating war at sea between England and Spain. When his relief ship finally reached Roanoke Island in 1590, White found the colony abandoned. There were no signs of a struggle, and the fate of the settlers remained a mystery. Some two decades later, however, rumors reached England from Virginia that the Roanoke Island colonists, finding their position on the island untenable, had journeyed north to the lower reaches of Chesapeake Bay. There, it was said, they had come upon friendly Indians and lived peacefully for many years, until the great chief Powhatan learned of their existence and ordered them annihilated. True or false, these reports attested to Powhatan's reputation

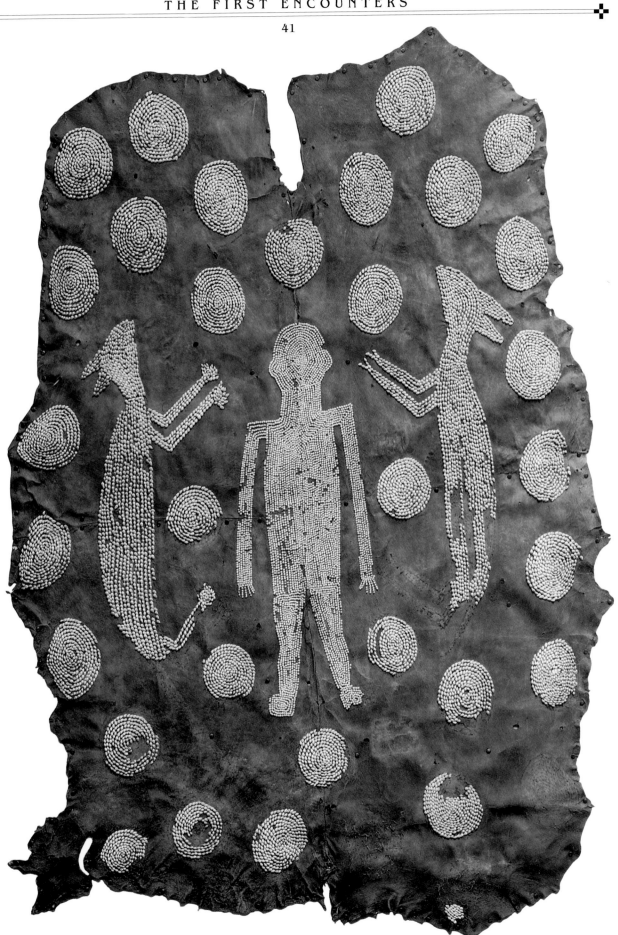

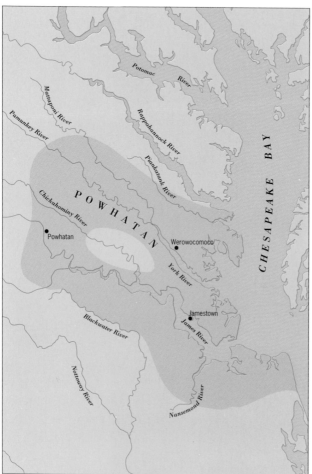

Powhatan's empire, which consisted of more than 30 Algonquian-speaking tribes, covered much of the area that is known as the Virginia Tidewater, extending south to the Great Dismal Swamp, north to the Rappahannock River, and inland as far as the falls of the main tidal rivers.

among the English, who were finding this proud native "king" to be as vexing an obstacle to their New World ambitions as any European monarch.

The English first made contact with Powhatan in 1607, when they established a new Virginia colony called Jamestown on an island in the lower James River, near Chesapeake Bay. This site put the 104 settlers just 12 or so miles south by land from Powhatan's capital of Werowocomoco, or Werowance Place, located on the York River. There Powhatan met with emissaries from the two dozen tribes he had subjugated since he had inherited control of several tribes along the upper James and York rivers as a young man several decades earlier. His personal empire, which extended north to the Rappahannock River and contained an estimated 14,000 subjects, had few if any parallels among native societies north of Mexico. Powhatan evidently feared no rivals among his own kind, but he may have harbored concerns about white intruders even before the founding of Jamestown. An Englishman reported that one of Powhatan's shamans, or holy men, had decreed that "bearded men should come and take away their country and that there should none of the original Indians be left, within a hundred and fifty years."

Powhatan was in his sixties when the Jamestown settlers arrived. Leaders of the infant colony who paid him court at Werowocomoco saw a tall sinewy man with long gray hair and wisps of beard sprouting from his chin. He was dressed like his male underlings in a plain deerskin breechcloth, moccasins, and raccoon cape. But seated on his elevated throne and ringed by his chief councilors, his bodyguard of 40 imposing bowmen, and the choicest of his 100 wives, he conveyed to one English emissary "such a majesty as I cannot express."

In their dealings with Powhatan, the settlers hoped to secure the same kind of aid sought by the hard-pressed colonists at Roanoke. The Jamestown contingent consisted of too few farmers and laborers and too many gentlemen and manservants who were diverted by futile forays for gold. As a result, the colony was in almost constant need of food for the first year or two of its existence. Powhatan was content to let his subjects

Having learned to smoke tobacco from the Indians, Europeans also copied the design of the Native Americans' clay pipes, one of which is shown at top. The English version (bottom) has a longer bowl and stem.

Evidence of early European influence on Indian ways, these two 17th-century containers were discovered near the site of the Jamestown settlement. The Indian clay jug at bottom mimics the European glass bottle at right with its round body and thin neck. The Virginia Indians made pottery in this shape only after the arrival of the English.

supply the settlers with corn and show them how to build fish weirs and plant vegetables in hills, Indian-style, in exchange for metal hatchets, glass beads, and copper. Part of this bounty found its way to Powhatan in the form of tribute, and he evidently hoped that Jamestown would serve as a trading post, furnishing him and his subordinates with goods that enhanced their status.

At the same time, he was intent on containing the English. Thus he sometimes looked the other way when one of his tribes harassed the settlers and stole their tools and weapons, and he staged an occasional deadly ambush of his own when he felt the intruders were out of line. Sometimes Indians would fail to appear at Jamestown to trade, and the colonists felt sure that the "subtle old fox," as one of them termed Powhatan, was behind it. Powhatan himself once reminded an English trading party through an interpreter that should they ever resort to intimidation, his people would hide their provisions "and fly to the woods, whereby you must famish."

The colony was made even more vulnerable by its unhealthy location amid bogs and marshes. In less than a year, dysentery, typhoid, and malnutrition carried away more than half the colonists. The survivors went out of their way to humor Powhatan. In September 1608, Captain Christo-

Dressed in European finery, Pocahontas, the daughter of Powhatan, sat for this portrait during her visit to England in 1616-1617 with her husband John Rolfe. She was about 21 years of age at the time and had taken the Christian name of Rebecca.

English dignitaries gave Pocahontas the cameo brooch above and the German stoneware jug at right. An observer noted that when meeting royalty at court, Pocahontas proudly "carried herself as the daughter of a king."

pher Newport, a former privateer who served the colony as president, presented the old chief with a copper crown and scarlet cloak and proclaimed him a special tributary to King James I. Powhatan reciprocated by giving Newport his raccoon cape and moccasins.

Captain John Smith, who was soon elected president in Newport's stead, had different ideas about handling the Indians. Such coddling, in his opinion, made Powhatan "much overvalue himself." A farmer's son turned soldier who had endured hard campaigns in Europe and North Africa, Smith cracked down on his colonists and their providers. To make the settlers less dependent, he put them all to work, even the gentlemen. Then, "to suppress the insolence of those proud savages," he organized raiding parties, which seized corn from villagers at gunpoint and repaid Indian attacks by burning houses and plundering burial places.

Alert to these deeds, Powhatan was relieved when Smith was injured by an exploding powder bag and forced to return to England, leaving the settlement at Jamestown without effective leadership. Having threatened previously to starve the colonists if they caused trouble, Powhatan now made good on his oath. As one settler put it, he "sent none of his Indians to trade with us but laid secret ambushes in the woods." Famine nearly wiped out Jamestown—a few of the settlers even resorted to cannibalism. Then in the summer of 1610, as the survivors were preparing to leave, hundreds of reinforcements arrived under the command of Sir Thomas Gates, a stern leader in Smith's mold. Backed by fresh troops, Gates set out to strip Powhatan of the support of local chiefs by making them pay tribute to the English instead. Those who refused risked having their crops taken and their children kidnapped. The captured youngsters were supposed to be raised as Christians, but the soldiers did not always observe this formality. In August English troops, having sacked a Paspahegh village on the James River and seized the chief's family, put his wife to the sword and dispatched his children, according to English officials, "by throwing them overboard and shooting out their brains in the water."

This grim campaign succeeded in loosening Powhatan's hold on his subjects. Along with the Indians who were forced into submission, a few tribes such as the Patawomeck—who lived along the south bank of the Potomac River—willingly cooperated with the English to gain trading favors and help cut Powhatan down to size. In April 1613, the werowance of the Patawomeck assisted in a plot to lure Powhatan's young daughter Pocahontas, who was a guest of the tribe at the time, aboard an English merchant ship. Once there, she was detained and held hostage. Under her captors' influence, she converted to Christianity and married planter John Rolfe. Outmaneuvered, Powhatan grudgingly acknowledged the union, thereby setting the stage for a truce.

In 1616 Pocahontas sailed for England to visit King James, accompanied by her husband, infant son, and 10 Powhatan councilors. One of those aides had been asked by Powhatan to tally the population of England on a notched stick, but soon grew "weary of that task," according to John Smith, who renewed his earlier acquaintance with Pocahontas at court. After creating a sensation there, she headed home with her party in March 1617, only to die suddenly on the way down the Thames River. Like so many of her people, she had fallen prey to some Old World disease.

Saddened and weary, Powhatan turned over power to his younger brother, Opechancanough, and died in 1618. The new werowance had to contend with an expanding Jamestown Colony, thanks in part to John Rolfe, who had introduced a mild strain of West Indian tobacco to Virginia in place of the bitter native variety. Exports of the crop helped trigger a smoking craze in England, despite King James's opposition to a habit he traced to "the barbarous and beastly manners of the wild, godless, and slavish Indians" and denounced as "hateful to the nose, harmful to the brain, dangerous to the lungs." The tobacco boom put new pressure on the Indians, for the crop depleted the soil, requiring new fields about every three years. By 1622 the colony was granting investors plantations of up to 80,000 acres— land obtained largely through deception or intimidation.

At the same time, the English launched a crusade to remake Indian culture. The objective, as the colony's secretary, William

Strachey, put it, was to change "their barbarous natures, make them ashamed the sooner of their savage nakedness, inform them of the true God, and of the way to their salvation, and finally teach them obedience to the king's majesty." To that end, the settlers started Christian schools for Indian children and even tried to win over Powhatan's successor, building him what one witness described as "a fair house after the English fashion," complete with a lock and key that so intrigued the chief he reportedly opened and closed it "a hundred times a day."

The English may have been amused by the idea of Opechancanough playing house, but he was not one to be bought off. Convinced that the expanding colony would soon overwhelm his people, he secretly rallied the demoralized elements of Powhatan's former empire and dealt a stunning blow to the intruders. On March 22, 1622, trusted Indians who were trading in English settlements, toiling for white planters in the fields, and even eating with them in their homes reached for the nearest hatchet or hoe and attacked, killing more than 300 men, women, and children—or nearly one-fourth of the colony's population.

During the uprising, Indians confiscated guns and ammunition, but they lacked the know-how to maintain the weapons for long (some rebels reportedly planted gunpowder like corn in the hope it would grow and increase). Once the English had recovered from the shock of the attack, they embarked on a long, methodical campaign of extermination that included burning crops and villages, chasing Indians down with dogs, and poisoning them with tainted peace offerings.

By the time Opechancanough conceded defeat and agreed to a truce with the English settlers in 1632, most of the surviving Indians had been driven inland to the Piedmont region, but that area too was now coveted by tobacco planters. Finally, in 1644, an aged Opechancanough—so infirm that he had to be carried about on a stretcher—launched another uprising on the frontier in the hope of stemming the white tide. Although 500 settlers died in the two-year rebellion, the colony was now 10,000 strong and could readily absorb such punishment and reply in kind. Within two years, the Indians were forced to accept a punitive treaty. Opechancanough himself died a prisoner in the Jamestown jail, where a soldier angered by the uprising shot him in the back.

Like the defiant chiefs of Florida, Powhatan and his successor had struggled against a destiny they could foresee but could never submit to. The shaman's old prophecy, that bearded men would come and steal their country, had been fulfilled. ❖

In a photograph taken in 1899, Pamunkey Indians of eastern Virginia—whose ancestors were once part of Powhatan's mighty empire—appear both in traditional garb, worn for show by the two men at left, and in the type of contemporary dress that most members of the tribe had adopted by this time.

LIFE IN A POWHATAN VILLAGE

Lush woodlands and plentiful waterways made the Virginia Tidewater a land of prosperity for the 30-odd Indian tribes known collectively as the Powhatan. The warm, humid climate and fertile soil provided rich harvests of corn, squash, and beans, and an abundance of wildlife made hunting and fishing relatively easy. In addition, the Chesapeake Bay offered annual bounties of mussels and oysters, while the surrounding oak and pine forests supplied nuts, wild roots, and berries. Unfortunately, few Powhatan artifacts have survived. The photographs here and on the following pages show a Powhatan village re-created at the Jamestown settlement near Williamsburg, Virginia. It depicts those villages existing in 1607 when the English established their first permanent colony in the Indians' domain.

The Powhatan built villages along the banks of the lower James River, shown here, and other waterways of the Chesapeake Bay region.

Carved images topped the wooden poles that the Powhatan arranged in circles for their ceremonial dances. The design for this effigy was based on the observations of an early English explorer.

The Powhatan built their lodges by fastening walls of dried bark or reed mats to frameworks of bent saplings. The walls were held together with cordage made from plant fibers and rawhide.

Sweat lodges were used for healing rituals. With the reed door rolled down, hot rocks rapidly heated the interior.

To make dugout canoes, the Powhatan burned holes in the center of logs, then scraped away the charred wood with shells like the ones shown here. The feather fan and blowpipe were used to maintain the fire.

To make their cloth-
ing, the Powhatan
stretched deer hides
on frames, rubbed
them with salt or
deer brains, and
then smoked them
over a fire to soften
them. For warm-
weather garments,
they removed the
fur with shell or
stone scrapers.

This hoe fashioned
from a conch shell
and these rakes and
digging tools made
from deer antlers
were the kinds of
implements used by
Powhatan women
for the cultivation of
their gardens.

A typical Powhatan village consisted of about 20 lodges situated among groves of trees and farmland.

The foods shown here—various beans, pecans, black walnuts, wild onions, wild strawberries, bayberry leaves, and dandelion greens—were staples of the Powhatan diet.

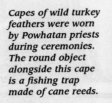

Capes of wild turkey feathers were worn by Powhatan priests during ceremonies. The round object alongside this cape is a fishing trap made of cane reeds.

A storage shelf is crowded with stone axes as well as scraping and garden tools made from bone. The clay cooking pots that are located below the shelf were reinforced with fragments of quartz or seashells.

Each growing season, the Powhatan sun-dried a portion of their harvest, such as these beans, for consumption during the winter months.

Spacious Powhatan lodges could accommodate up to 20 family members. Typically, they slept on platforms lining the walls.

2

A map dated 1546 depicts the New World according to a description by the French explorer Jacques Cartier. The view, from the north, takes in Canada's present-day Maritime Provinces with the Atlantic coastline extending upward. Cartier is pictured in a short black robe standing with colonists and Canadian Indians who are wearing fur. Cartier and other explorers returned to Europe with curios such as this 17th-century Huron box (above).

CONFLICT IN THE NORTH WOODS

In 1497, five years after Columbus fetched up on the islands of the Caribbean in his bid to open a new sea route to the Indies, a mariner named John Cabot reconnoitered at high latitudes with the same goal. Like Columbus, Cabot—born Giovanni Caboto—was an ambitious Genoa native who offered his skills abroad. Backed by England's King Henry VII, he and 18 crewmen had set out from Bristol in a small ship in late May, sailing westward in search of the palaces and spice ports of the Orient. Instead, about one month into their journey, they came upon a desolate shore whose dark forests stretched away without limit.

Acutely aware of the puniness of his force against this immense backdrop, Cabot landed only briefly. He and his men stayed just long enough to erect a cross and raise the English banner before continuing along the coast. They headed home a month or so later with a vague idea that this seeming wilderness, which Cabot dubbed Newfoundland, was home to a strange race. As a dispatch written after their return put it: "They found a trail that went inland, they saw a site where a fire had been made, they saw manure of animals that they thought to be farm animals. All along the coast they found many fish like those which in Iceland are dried in the open and sold in England and other countries. And thus following the shore, they saw two forms running on land one after the other, but they could not tell if they were human beings or animals."

The sight of ambiguous "forms" in the distance was perplexing for the explorers, as it must have been for those running figures if they in turn had looked out to sea and spotted mysterious creatures atop the high-sterned carrack horsing its way through the waves. Such cryptic perceptions of an alien existence would prove to be sadly prophetic, for the natives of the Old World and the inhabitants of this newfound land would remain enigmas to each other even when the tide of events brought them face to face. Between the two camps lay a chasm so wide that it bred incomprehension, so deep that each side sometimes had cause to question the other's humanity. The two parties would be ill met.

The cultural confrontation along the northern frontier of the New World did not originate with Cabot's voyage. As early as the 11th century, hardy Norsemen sailing from settlements on Iceland had begun exploring the coasts of Greenland, Labrador, and Newfoundland, making a fearful impression on the native peoples that would endure in their folklore. More recently, small bands of European fishermen—a tight-knit fraternity who kept their knowledge to themselves—may have been exploiting the prolific waters of the Grand Banks, within sight of Newfoundland. But Cabot's well-publicized expedition lifted any secrecy shrouding the fishing grounds, and soon men were making the journey in droves—from England, Brittany, Normandy, Portugal, and the Basque country between France and Spain. Often leaving their home ports in the dead of winter, they braved the gale-wracked, ice-strewn North Atlantic to harvest cod and other fish with net and hook and speed back home by June, sometimes returning the same summer to fill their holds again.

As Europeans came to depend on cod as a staple of their diet, the value of the North American catch rivaled that of all the precious metals pouring into Spain from the New World. Throughout the 16th century, the fishing industry would grow, and the coastal contacts it spurred between Europeans and Native Americans would give rise to a new and even bigger business—the fur trade. In the 17th century, that trade would spread deep into the northern interior via the Saint Lawrence, Connecticut, and Hudson rivers. And with the commerce came calamity—fierce new intertribal rivalries, an erosion of self-sufficiency, and waves of epidemic disease that weakened native societies, endangering an ancient way of life delicately attuned to the rhythms and resources of the woodlands.

The Northeast at the time of the European onslaught was home to dozens of tribes that sometimes battled fiercely with one another but were linked by trade, language, and custom. Like the Indians encountered by the English around Roanoke Island and Jamestown, most northeastern peoples spoke versions of the huge language family known as Algonquian. The ranks of Algonquian speakers included the Montagnais of Labrador and eastern Quebec; the Micmac in Nova Scotia and environs; the Abenaki of Maine; and, directly in the path of the future white settlers of New England, such tribes as the Pawtucket, Massachusett, Wampanoag, Narragansett, and Pequot. Farther inland lived members of another language family, the Iroquoian; these groups included the powerful Huron of what is now southern Ontario and, in a wide band stretching across central New York, the five allied tribes of the Iroquois League—the Mohawk, Oneida, Onondaga, Cayuga, and Seneca.

Leadership within the various Indian communities of the region generally was vested in honored individuals whose authority rested on their powers of persuasion. Unlike the proud paramounts of the Mississippian tradition, these headmen—known as sachems among the New England tribes—could not simply impose their will. They had to seek a consensus, relying on their eloquence and their reputation for wisdom or bravery; and even then, the decisions were not always binding on individuals. This consensual approach to government applied at all levels, including the deliberations of the Iroquois League, a political structure that gained great weight as difficulties with the white men grew. Each year, the tribes that made up the Iroquois confederacy sent chiefs to a great council. Any decision reached there had to be of "one heart, one mind, one law." Barring that, the matter was put aside and the council fire covered with ashes.

If allies sometimes found it hard to agree, ancestral rivals were seldom able to overcome their differences, and warfare was chronic in the Northeast. Traditionally, men fought not to subjugate villages or seize territory but to win glory and avenge the latest stroke in a blood feud whose origins lay beyond memory. The Iroquois viewed battle as the supreme source of personal prestige and made it part of their seasonal cycle, with war parties of 500 men or more setting out in spring and summer to seize

CONTACTS WITH THE NORSEMEN

Hundreds of years before John Cabot and his contemporaries landed on the shores of eastern Canada, Indians in that part of North America had encountered Norse seafarers. The first of these early explorers reached the northern tip of Newfoundland about AD 1000 where they attempted to establish a westward extension of the Greenland colony founded by Erik the Red. Norse and Inuit sagas recount isolated contacts between the two peoples. Testifying to such linkage is the driftwood sculpture at left, just over two inches high, discovered in the remains of a 13th-century Inuit house on Baffin Island, Canada. Although the stubby arms and blank face are typical of Inuit carvings of the day, the figure's European-style cloak with a cross incised on its chest identifies it as a Norseman, perhaps a visitor who came ashore to trade.

Photographed in 1854, a Micmac mother and son wear clothing that reflects more than three centuries of French influence. The Micmac, an Algonquian-speaking tribe occupying Nova Scotia and adjacent areas, were among the first native people to meet 15th- and 16th-century European fishermen who set up bases along the Atlantic shore.

captives from the rival Huron or other hostile tribes—sorties that virtually guaranteed retaliation. If a war party had to make a hasty retreat, prisoners were often killed on the spot and sometimes scalped or beheaded. The fate of captives who reached the victors' village varied. Women and children were usually adopted by families that had lost members in war. Male prisoners were generally executed, but only after they had been tortured—their flesh burned and cut and sometimes even eaten in a protracted rite that the victim tried to endure bravely, singing his death song.

Yet warfare was not an all-absorbing activity. Even the most aggressive tribes confined their raids to the proper seasons and engaged in equitable trade with neighboring groups. The exchanges sometimes involved necessities such as food or hides, but much trade revolved around luxury items—beads, shells, or porcupine quills, used to decorate ceremonial clothing and ritual objects. Although such objects were treasured, there was little to be gained by hoarding great quantities in this life or the next—few tribes in the region staged lavish burial rites of the sort accorded the Mississippian chiefs. Before European values took hold, trade was regarded not as a competitive exercise but as a reciprocal activity, one that often served to ease tensions between communities or seal alliances.

Most peoples of the Northeast earned their livelihood through a mixture of hunting, gathering, and horticulture, although farming was of less importance in areas where the growing season was short, and no crops at all were raised in the far north. In southern New England, as in other fertile areas, most of the agricultural labor was done by women, who worked the soil with hoes that might be tipped with the shells of clams or turtles, or crafted from the shoulder blade of a deer. Like their counterparts around the Virginia colonies, the women heaped up small mounds of earth every four feet or so and planted a few kernels of corn in each hill, along with a similar number of beans, which would climb up the cornstalks as they grew. Squash and tubers were also cultivated, but the region's staple was corn, consumed in the form of gruel, hominy, or cakes. Typically, a woman produced about 15 bushels of grain a year.

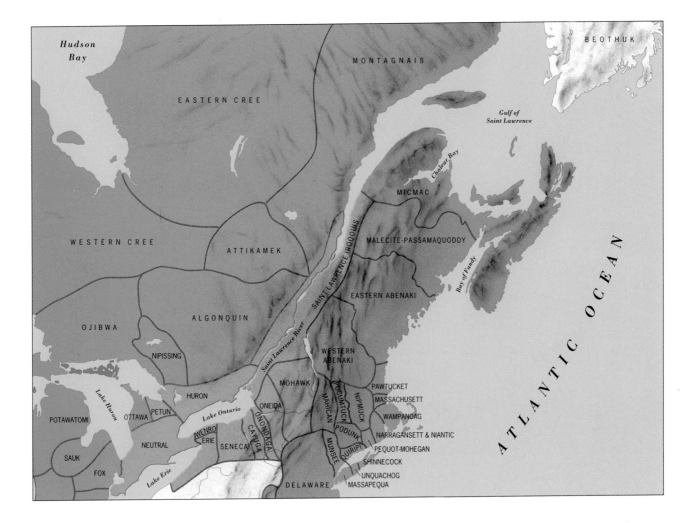

Europeans of the 17th century made contact with scores of tribes in northeastern Canada and what is now the United States. In general, Algonquian-speaking peoples (green) lived in a wedge of territory along the Atlantic Coast and an area around the Great Lakes, while Iroquoian-speaking cultures (red) occupied the area comprising present-day upstate New York, part of Ontario, and the Saint Lawrence River valley.

Farther north, among maritime groups such as the Micmac of Nova Scotia, little was grown other than tobacco. Crops might be obtained through trade with tribes to the south, but most food was procured from the wild according to an immemorial schedule. In January, men ventured out in canoes to kill seals breeding on offshore islands; the fat was rendered for body grease and cooking oil, and the fur was woven by women into clothing. In March, spawning smelt thronged the rivers, followed by herring, sturgeon, and salmon. Trapped in weirs or speared, the fish supplemented the ongoing harvest of mollusks, gathered along the shore for much of the year. Through the spring, waterfowl arrived and nested, offering a ready supply of eggs. In the summer, beaver were speared or shot with bows after their dams had been destroyed, and geese were targeted

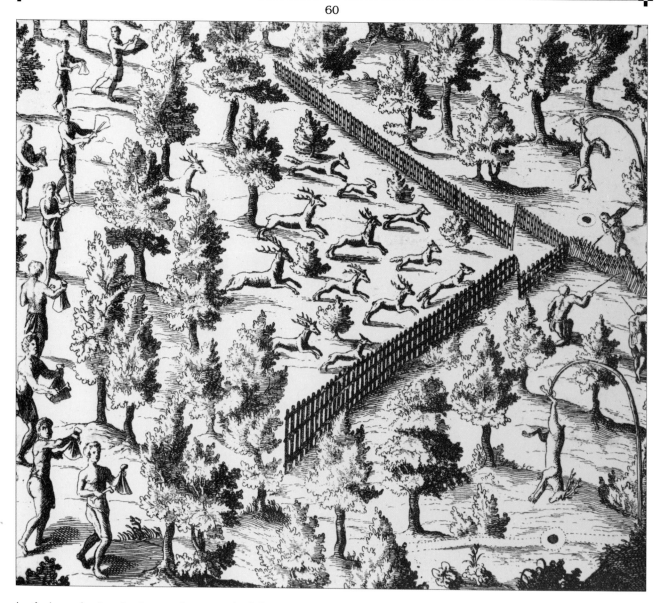

in their rookeries. In September, people followed spawning eels upriver. When the leaves fell, small hunting parties left the seashore with their dogs and moved up the region's many rivers into the woods to track caribou, black bear, and—best of all—moose, prized not only for its savory meat but also for its hide and antlers, which yielded clothing, tent coverings, tools, and ornaments. Then the annual round began again.

Other patterns prevailed among the Indians of the interior. The Huron, living along the upper Saint Lawrence and the eastern Great Lakes, were skillful farmers as well as foragers, cultivating fields of corn and beans that covered up to 60 acres. Despite enrichment from the ash of a yearly burning-over, a field had to be abandoned after eight to 10 years; new ones were created by cutting or girdling trees to kill them, then torching the deadwood. The Iroquois practiced similar slash-and-burn farming to supplement their bountiful hunting expeditions, which yielded each tribal group as many as 2,000 deer annually.

In a drawing from a book by French explorer Samuel de Champlain, Huron beaters drive deer into a trap where they will be dispatched by spear-wielding hunters. Other deer are taken with snares. Champlain noted that "there is great sport in such hunting," and added that the Huron regard it "as the most noble form of the chase."

Not even the region's most productive farmers lived in one place all year. People moved with the seasonal availability of wild foods—to fishing or fowling camps, hunting grounds, and places where nuts or berries abounded. Settlements also had to be shifted as fields gave out. The New England Indians were dispersed in small villages or even solitary houses; their typical family dwelling was the wigwam—a round structure, about 12 feet in diameter, formed by covering a bent-sapling framework with sheets of bark or mats woven from leaves, rushes, or cattails. The Huron and Iroquois had a denser pattern of settlement. Related families lived in long houses—bark-covered structures about 25 feet wide and often more than 100 feet long. Villages ranged in size from a few long houses to a hundred or more. Some towns had more than 1,000 inhabitants and were fortified with double or triple palisades.

Such large settlements were the exception. The Northeast was sparsely populated compared to the temperate Southeast, with its long growing season. Vast expanses of forest were empty, unfit for farming and visited only for seasonal hunting or fishing. Yet tribes were aware of their territory and deeply attached to it. Land was not to be exploited or exchanged. It was part of the enveloping spirit world—from which the plants and animals drew their powers. Before strangers altered the terms they lived by, the inhabitants would no more think of selling land than of trading away the air they breathed.

The Europeans, for their part, were intent on staking claims and extracting wealth from the region.

Huron women, responsible for the tribe's agricultural work, boil maple syrup (foreground) and plant corn in this 18th-century French engraving. While maize was a staple food for these Indians, accounting for about 65 percent of their diet, maple sugar was a prized seasoning, often used in place of salt to enhance the flavor of various foods.

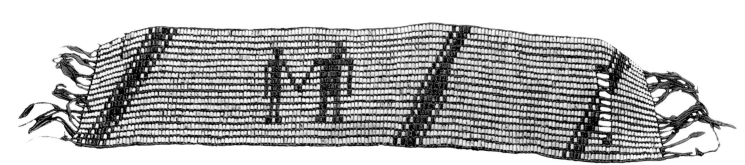

Within a few decades of Cabot's voyage in 1497, the inhabitants of coastal Newfoundland, Labrador, and Nova Scotia were being visited by fishermen from several countries, who put ashore for fresh water and firewood and likely traded with the Indians in the process. At first, these fishermen preserved their cod for the return trip by salting it on board. But as demand increased for this so-called beef of the sea—which fed Europe's armies and navies, its lower classes, and most of its Catholics on the holy days when meat was forbidden—the crews freed up space on their ships by curing the fish at camps onshore. These stations, together with whaling bases along the Gulf of Saint Lawrence, became beachheads where Europeans secured a footing in the New World and learned of other assets such as furs that would draw them deep into the interior.

Meanwhile, explorers following in Cabot's wake continued to seek a profitable route to the Indies across the North Atlantic. Among those taking up the quest were the sea-wise Portuguese. Alarmed by Cabot's thrust, they sent a nobleman named Gaspar Côrte-Real across the ocean at high latitudes in the year 1500. He too came up against the formidable barrier of Newfoundland, which he described tersely as "a land that is very cool and with big trees." Returning to the area the following year, his

A beaded belt showing a European in a broad-brimmed hat and a Native American holding hands commemorates a 1682 treaty of friendship between the Delaware Indians and William Penn, founder of the Pennsylvania Colony.

An Abenaki powder horn from Maine is incised with typical Native American designs as well as a European-style meeting house. European soldiers introduced the Abenaki to horns for carrying gunpowder.

expedition landed on the southern coast of Newfoundland. Côrte-Real pushed westward in search of the passage to Asia and was lost at sea. The crews of his remaining two ships made it back to Portugal, where they told of encountering people who lived "by fishing and hunting animals, in which the land abounds, such as very large deer, covered with extremely long hair, the skins of which they use for garments and also make houses and boats thereof." Notwithstanding their many uses, these long-haired "deer"—probably caribou—seemed a poor thing to the Portuguese compared to the wealth of the Orient. By way of consolation, they brought back 57 natives and sold them as slaves.

Thereafter, the Portuguese shifted their attention to the south, but others were eager to pursue the path they abandoned. In 1524 the French commissioned a Florentine navigator named Giovanni da Verrazano to explore the northern latitudes of America in search of a passage to the Pacific—the ocean that, thanks to recent Portuguese maritime feats, was now known to separate the New World from the Indies. Probing for an inlet, Verrazano entered the harbor below the island of Manhattan, where in his words, Indians on the shore gestured "toward us with evident delight, raising loud shouts of admiration." But a strong wind forced him to weigh anchor without making contact, and he continued along the south shore of Long Island to Narragansett Bay. The Indians he met there were evidently familiar with Europeans: They possessed some wrought-copper plates, presumably acquired in trade. Those dealings must have been friendly, since they greeted the explorers with "real signs of joy, bringing us provisions and signifying to us where we could best ride in safety."

Verrazano then proceeded to Maine, where he encountered the Abenaki, whose attitude toward Europeans was quite different. "If we wished at any time to traffic with them," Verrazano wrote, "they came to the seashore and stood upon the rocks, from which they lowered down by a cord to our boats beneath whatever they had to barter, continually crying out to us not to come nearer and instantly demanding from us that which was to be given in exchange; they took from us only knives, fishhooks, and sharpened steel. No regard was paid to our courtesies; when we had nothing left to exchange with them, the men at our departure made the most brutal signs of disdain and contempt possible."

Having failed to locate a passage to the Pacific, Verrazano devoted the rest of his exploring career to southern latitudes, where he came to a grim end: He was killed and eaten by Carib cannibals in 1528. But his

A Seneca antler comb found in western New York depicts a small dog and a European gripping a musket and wearing a buttoned jacket and pantaloons. Although Indian women had used combs long before the arrival of the Europeans, designs such as this reflected the influence of white settlers.

A family of Montagnais Indians, named after the French word for mountaineer because of the steep terrain where they lived, stands with a canoe on the shore of a bay in Labrador in the 1890s. As the European fur trade depleted the stocks of moose, elk, and beaver, the Montagnais increasingly turned to fish for food, especially trout and salmon.

coastal investigations had given France a claim to North America, and in 1534 the government sent Jacques Cartier, a Breton mariner, across the Atlantic to solidify it, and perhaps discover that elusive route to the Orient in the process—a mission that led to the first sustained contact between Europeans and native peoples of present-day Canada. Heading across the Atlantic in late spring, Cartier's two ships threaded the strait between Newfoundland and Labrador and entered the Gulf of Saint Lawrence. Cartier was far from impressed by the scraggly terrain he glimpsed, and he concluded that this was the dismal land that "God appointed for Cain." The impression was reinforced by the first Indians he encountered, whom he characterized as "wild and intractable," in part because of their fierce appearance—they wore red body paint and arranged their hair atop their heads "like a wreath of hay, stuck through with a wooden pin." As Cartier conceded, however, these "wild" Indians—Algonquian speakers whom the French later dubbed the Montagnais—were adept at the art of survival in an infertile land, harvesting "great quantities of seals" in the gulf from their birch-bark canoes before moving on to the next stop in their seasonal round. And as future French visitors would confirm, they were eager to trade with Indians and white men alike.

Continuing to the south and west, Cartier reached the Gaspé Peninsula in July where he met with a large party of Indians who had ventured far from their home base near the future city of Quebec to fish in the gulf. The men of the party welcomed the French in the traditional fashion with songs and dances, while the women waited in the woods, with the exception of two or three who came forward cautiously to greet the visitors. Cartier noted that the captain of his ship gave each of the women "a comb and a small tin bell, with which they were much delighted, showing their gratitude to our captain by rubbing his breast and arms with their hands. The reception of these presents occasioned all the other women to return from the wood, that they might likewise participate; for which purpose they surrounded the captain, to the number of about 20, touching and rubbing him with their hands, as soliciting him for such trinkets as he had given the others. He accordingly gave each of them a small bell, on which they all fell asinging and dancing."

Cartier was impressed by the stores of food these people had brought with them from their home fields, including corn, beans, figs, and other fruit—signs that the region might one day reward French settlement. But his interest was in finding a passage to the Pacific, and in late July, he prepared to continue the search, erecting a large cross on a hill to mark

Three 17th-century drawings, among the earliest and most accurate pictures of woodlands Indians, depict chiefs holding smoking pipes. All illustrate the importance of body decoration in the region, especially the Iroquois (lower right). His turtle and snake tattoos probably represent spirit guides that had appeared to him in a vision.

their anchorage. Alarmed by this, the chief of the party, Donnacona, approached the French vessels in a canoe with his brother and sons and delivered a stern oration to the visitors in his native tongue, "pointing frequently to our cross, and making a cross with his two fingers; he then pointed out to all the country round about, as if showing that all was his, and that we must not erect any more crosses without his leave."

The French pacified the chief by taking his party aboard and treating them to food and drink. Cartier then indicated through gestures that he meant to carry two of Donnacona's sons along on the next leg of the voyage and bring them back in due time. To signal his intentions, he clothed the youngsters "in shirts and colored coats, with red caps, putting a copper chain around each of their necks, with which they seemed much pleased, and remained willingly along with us." Donnacona accepted this, perhaps because it was customary in his culture for allies and trading partners to exchange children for a time as tokens of good faith.

Once embarked, the two boys had no choice but to accompany their hosts back to France, for after searching in vain for a westward passage, Cartier and his men decided not to risk wintering in the area and headed home. The youths soon learned enough French to communicate with Cartier, and what they told him of their native land made him eager to return. Beyond their tribal territory—which they called Canada—lay a body of fresh water so extensive that no man they knew of had ever traveled to the end of it. This was evidently a reference to Lake Ontario, but Cartier, ignorant of the vast extent of the American interior, hoped that it might prove to be the coveted passage to the Orient. The following summer, he returned to the New World with an expedition of three ships. Helped by his young guides, he located the broad mouth of the Saint Lawrence River and proceeded upstream. In early September, they reached the village of Stadacona—Donnacona's seat near present-day Quebec city—where the boys were reunited with their father. Although he warmly embraced Cartier, the chief was reluctant to assist him in his plans to explore farther up the river, fearing that he would form an alliance with a rival tribe. Donnacona's sons declined to rejoin the expedition, as Cartier had hoped, and he had to carry on without them.

Although autumn was closing in, Cartier struggled up the Saint Lawrence in a pinnace for two more weeks, reaching a palisaded Indian settlement called Hochelaga at the base of a lofty hill, almost 1,000 miles from the Atlantic. He named the hill Mont Réal—site of the future French city. From its crest, he could see rapids upriver and concluded that the route was all but impassable. He therefore returned to winter near Stadacona at a fort his men had prepared. Amid the snow and ice, relations between the two sides deteriorated. The two boys who had visited France knew the slight value the visitors put on the items they were trading to the Indians and urged their people to ask more for the food they brought to market. As the months wore on and the visitors grew hungrier, the Indians did just that, sometimes carrying their fish and venison home unsold rather than accepting what Cartier's men offered them. Donnacona himself continued to assist the French, however. When he learned in March that Cartier's men were suffering from scurvy, he drew on his native lore and taught the French how to brew a tea from cedar fronds that cured the sufferers within a week. Despite such charity, Cartier was conscious of his vulnerable position and always on the lookout for signs that the chief was turning against him. When local rivals to Donnacona fanned these French suspicions, Cartier took a drastic step. In early May, he lured Donnacona, his two boys, and seven other prominent Indians to the fort, took them hostage, and abruptly sailed with them for France. Cartier evidently hoped that the chief's rivals would be grateful for this stroke and welcome the French with open arms when they came back to colonize the area. But when Cartier finally returned with such an expedition six years later—by which time Donnacona and all but one of his fellow hostages had died—the new chief of Stadacona cautiously distanced himself from the people who had betrayed his predecessor. After two years of disputes and sporadic skirmishing, the colony collapsed, and the survivors headed home for good.

For the Indians of the region, the chief legacy of such early, fitful encounters was disease. Various ills were communicated by members of Cartier's expedition and fishermen trading with Indians at their coastal bases. In all, perhaps 10 major epidemics surged inland from the European contact points like tidal waves during the 16th century. And the devastation only increased thereafter, as white men appeared in greater numbers and delved deeper into the region.

What lured most of those intruders was not the elusive treasures of the Orient—although some navigators still dreamed of finding a passage to the Pacific—but assets that were closer at hand and every bit as rewarding: furs. Early on, the New World fur trade was a lucrative sideline for fishermen and explorers, who brought back small pelts that could be made into hand muffs, collars, borders, and other forms of luxurious trim for Europe's upper classes. Fox, lynx, ermine, otter, raccoon, and marten all were suitable, but the choice pelt was that of the rare black fox; in 1584 one of these shimmering, ebony skins fetched 100 pounds at market in London. Toward the end of the century, interest in another sleek material accelerated the fur trade and provided a prime motive for ventures to America. Broad-brimmed felt hats became the rage in Europe, and the best material for the purpose was the soft, dark, finely barbed underfur of the beaver. By 1600 the beaver was almost extinct in Europe. The American Northeast, by contrast, had a seemingly endless supply of the animals, and the colder climate endowed them with thicker fur.

The Indians had long hunted beaver for their pelts, which they wove into cloaks and other articles, but since the animals were widely distributed across the Northeast, their fur was not a major trade item. Now the region's inhabitants found that beaver pelts would bring them what they wanted most from the white man. Although they would sometimes accept glass beads, mirrors, and other alluring items in exchange for the furs, the Indians put a premium on two useful materials that were rare or nonexistent in the Northeast—metal and cloth. (Some copper was mined by Indians around Lake Superior, and silver in northern Quebec, but the region as a whole was devoid of cotton and other textile fibers.) Indian traders coveted metal in the form of knives, axes, and hatchets. In addition, they valued copper or brass either in sheets or in the form of kettles, which could then be cut and hammered into ornaments such as bracelets, rings, pendants, and bangles. Together with wool and cotton, these items defined the Europeans for the Indians, who referred to the newcomers variously as "knife-men," "iron-men," or "cloth-men."

The Dutch and the English competed for their share of the American fur business, but French traders made the greatest impact. Following in Cartier's path, French merchant ships in the late 1500s traveled up the Saint Lawrence to the Indian trading center of Tadoussac, at the terminus

Armed with muskets and bows, northeastern Indians besiege an imaginatively rendered beaver lodge in this 1760 Italian engraving. Before they acquired guns, some tribes hunted beaver during the winter by destroying their lodges and killing the animals when they were forced to come up to holes in the ice to breathe. Other tribes trapped the coveted animals.

LA CACCIA DEI CASTORI.

Winding through central Quebec, the Saguenay River looks much as it did when the French first began to trade with the Montagnais Indians there in the late 16th century. An early French explorer dismissed the surrounding landscape as "nothing but mountains and promontories of rock—a country disagreeable from whatever point of view."

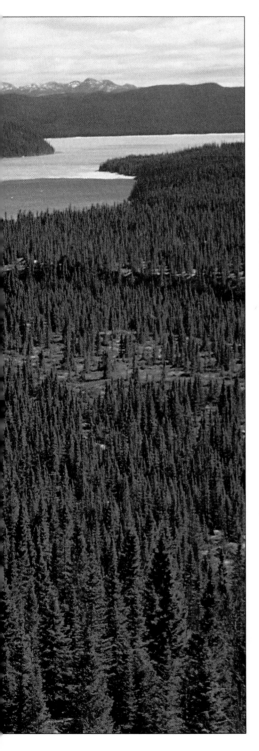

of the Saguenay River, roughly two-thirds of the way between the Gaspé Peninsula and the site where Cartier had wintered. Native traders had long converged at Tadoussac bearing goods from the northern interior, the Maritime Provinces, and the Great Lakes region. Now the site became the focus of a fur trade that was to transform the lives of Indians throughout the area. Among the first to feel the effects were the Montagnais, who dominated Tadoussac and the lower Saguenay. They became middlemen, receiving beaver pelts from occupants of the interior and passing them on to the French in exchange for metal, cloth, and other wares.

This new role brought the Montagnais material rewards and prestige. But it also distracted them from their traditional foraging activities. If food ran short, of course, they could always trade pelts for provisions from the willing French. Elsewhere, other Indians near French trading posts were already developing a taste for dried peas and cod, biscuits, and other preserved foods, which they obtained by gathering furs at the expense of fish and game. Once such groups lost the knack for arduous hunting and fishing expeditions, they seldom regained it. By the early 1600s, some smaller tribes that had been largely self-sufficient were getting much of their food from the Europeans or from other native groups through trade. Meanwhile, handicrafts were being neglected as well, since European wares could be readily obtained for pelts. As one Montagnais trader explained to a Frenchman: "The beaver does everything perfectly well. It makes kettles, hatchets, swords, knives, bread. In short, it makes everything."

The pitfalls of dependency were not immediately apparent to the Indians entranced by European goods. Of more pressing concern for the Montagnais and others who dealt directly with the fur traders was the jealousy their privileged position inspired in rival groups who lacked access to the foreigners. The Mohawk and their Iroquois League allies, whose territory lay south of the Saint Lawrence, coveted French wares—above all metal weapons that were sturdier than traditional stone blades and points—and they stepped up raids on their northern rivals accordingly. Their goal, apparently, was to drive those groups away and deal with the white men themselves. In 1603 when members of a French fur-trading expedition ventured up the Saint Lawrence beyond Tadoussac in search of Stadacona, Hochelaga, and other native settlements visited by Cartier, they found the area all but abandoned. Those few Indians the French met spoke fearfully of the Iroquois, who had reportedly launched attacks of unusual severity that dispersed whole villages. To counter the Iroquois, the Montagnais around Tadoussac had recently begun to seek

Prior to the arrival of European traders with iron tools and firearms, Indians relied on local resources for their weaponry. It is likely that Iroquois warriors used this 17th-century tomahawk, fitted with an inlaid wooden haft and stone blade, to scalp their enemies.

alliances with other Algonquian-speaking peoples in the vicinity, forming war parties in excess of 1,000 men.

Thus far, the French had steered clear of these disputes. But that changed under the leadership of Samuel de Champlain, a soldier and cartographer who took part in the 1603 expedition and returned to the area in 1608 with a royal charter to found a permanent French trading post on the Saint Lawrence. Arriving at Tadoussac in June of that year, he won permission from the Montagnais to establish his colony upriver, at the site called Quebec, near the ruins of the fort occupied by Cartier. After building some houses there and surrounding them with a protective palisade and a broad ditch, the colonists planted wheat, rye, and other European crops in the hope of attaining self-sufficiency. Champlain found that tensions were still running at a fever pitch between the Iroquois and the Algonquian allies, and he concluded that the French would have to intervene if they hoped to move their goods freely along the Saint Lawrence. He cast his lot with the Algonquians—in part because they were already trusted trading partners of the French and in part because their suppliers to the north provided beaver pelts that were thicker than those available to the south.

After a cruel winter that cost many lives, Champlain mustered 20 or so French soldiers and headed south with an Algonquian war party. That July they clashed with Iroquois warriors—probably Mohawk—along the shores of the lake that would later bear Champlain's name. The Iroquois carried wooden shields, which served well against arrows but offered scant protection against the muskets wielded by the French. Champlain himself loaded his ponderous weapon with several bullets, aimed it at three chiefs who were leading the Iroquois forward, and felled two of them with a single blast. Unaccustomed to gunfire, their followers turned and fled, leaving behind several dead and perhaps a dozen prisoners.

That night, Champlain looked on as the Algonquians berated one of the captives and prepared to torture him in the traditional manner. "They ordered him to sing, if he had the heart," Champlain reported. "He did so, but it was a very sad song to hear." The ordeal—which included burning, piercing, and scalping—appalled Champlain, who was invited to participate but tried to make the Algonquians understand that the French "did not commit such cruelties." In fact, tortures such as evisceration and burning at the stake were still being practiced in Europe at that time, albeit on heretics and traitors rather than prisoners of war. Finally, Champlain was allowed to shoot the captive and end his torment.

The following summer, in June of 1610, Champlain aided the Algonquians in another successful strike against the Iroquois along the Richelieu River, north of Lake Champlain. For all the shock effect of the French firearms, however, the actions Champlain took part in were basically raids of retribution, and they did not remove the Iroquois as a threat to French interests. Soon, Champlain found himself embroiled in further conflict. In 1615 he ventured up the Saint Lawrence to visit the Huron, who dominated the headwaters of that river and the northern shore of Lake Ontario. Although the Huron spoke an Iroquoian dialect, they had maintained good relations with their Algonquian trading partners along the river while feuding bitterly with the Iroquois to their south.

Impressed by the bustling Huron villages and their well-tended fields, Champlain hoped that by adding this energetic people to the list of French allies, he would keep the Iroquois at bay and extend the range of French trade. To that end, he joined the Huron in an attack on a fortified Iroquois village in September. Once again, however, he found that his Indian co-

Samuel de Champlain, accompanied by Algonquian allies and supported by two French musketeers, defeats a raiding party of Mohawk Iroquois at the southern tip of Lake Champlain on July 29, 1609, in the first recorded encounter of the Iroquois with European firearms. Although the skirmish secured Champlain's alliance with Algonquians, he made bitter enemies of the powerful Iroquois League's Five Nations.

TEE YEE NEEN HO GA ROW   SA GA YEATH QUA PIETH TOW

horts were more interested in sparring with their rivals and taking prisoners than in dealing them a crushing blow. When he urged the Huron to set fire to the fortifications, they declined. Instead, they waited for Iroquois warriors to emerge from the fort and skirmished with them. After collecting a dozen or more captives, they headed home with their trophies.

Discouraged by this foray, Champlain abandoned the warpath for good and returned to Quebec to watch over the struggling colony of New France, which was slowly assimilating Indians in the area through intermarriage, trading obligations, and the mission work of Jesuit priests, some of whom ranged deep into Huron country in search of converts. Once the French had fanned the intertribal conflict, however, it took on a destructive momentum of its own. Alarmed by the recent attacks, the Iroquois grew more determined to prevent their rivals from enjoying exclusive access to European goods and the power those goods conferred.

Recently, traders from another Old World country had approached Iroquois territory from the south. In 1609 the English navigator Henry Hudson, sailing under Dutch colors, had ventured past Manhattan and probed 150 miles up the waterway that would be known thenceforth as the Hudson River. There he bargained with the local Algonquian-

HO NEE YEATH TAW NO ROW

ETOW OH KOAM

Paintings of four sachems, or chiefs, three Mohawk and one Mahican (far right), depict the leaders in combinations of European cloaks and Indian trappings against a wild forest background. The portraits were commissioned when the delegation visited Queen Anne of England in 1710 as part of an effort by English colonial leaders to generate Crown support for the border struggle with the French. The ranking chief of the group (far left) holds a wampum belt, similar to one that he presented to the queen.

speaking Mahican for furs. When word of his coup reached Amsterdam, Dutch traders leaped into action, establishing a post called Fort Nassau on a flood-prone island in the upper Hudson. In 1623 a new trading post called Fort Orange was built a few miles away, at present-day Albany.

The Dutch hoped to continue dealing with Mahicans, whom Hudson had characterized as "loving people" and easy trading partners. But the Mohawk, whose territory lay a short distance north of Fort Orange, had other ideas. They went on the attack, and not even the support of Dutchmen brandishing firearms could prevent their Mahican allies from being swept away. Suddenly, the traders found themselves dealing with Indians who were "stronger than ourselves," as one Dutch colonist put it. To complicate matters, the Mohawk forbade hostile tribes to their north to pass through their territory, which meant that prime Canadian beaver pelts could not reach Fort Orange except through Iroquois middlemen. But the Dutch made the best of the situation, recognizing that the Mohawk and their fellow Iroquois allies could be used as a wedge against the French and their Indian trading partners along the Saint Lawrence. To that end, the Dutch concluded an alliance with the Mohawk in 1643 and began to provide them firearms in trade for furs. A single provocative exchange in 1648 brought the Mohawk 400 muskets. Thus equipped, they and their Iroquois partners, the Seneca, trained their sights on their Huron enemies to the north.

This challenge could not have come at a worse time for the Huron. In recent decades, they had emerged as the leading fur suppliers to the French, providing up to 12,000 pelts a year that were relayed by Indian traders from as far away as Hudson Bay. In return, however, the Huron had to put up with the presence of the Jesuits, who spread disease and discord along with the word of God. A series of epidemics between 1635 and 1641 reduced the Huron population from around 20,000 to scarcely half that. As a Jesuit missionary noted, the situation was aggravated by the absence of any sort of quarantine: "The Huron—no matter what plague or contagion they may have—live in the midst of their sick as if they were in perfect health. In a few days, almost all those in the cabin of the deceased found themselves infected; then the evil spread from house to house, from village to village." Another Jesuit reported that some Huron converts blamed their plight on the priests and angrily abandoned the faith, asserting that "their baptism was at once followed by every possible misfortune. The Dutch, they say, have preserved the Iroquois by allowing them to live in their own fashion, just as the black gowns have ruined the Huron by preaching the faith to them."

Greater misfortune lay in store for the people. In the spring of 1649, more than 1,000 Mohawk and Seneca warriors, well stocked with firearms, carried out a string of attacks on Huron villages aimed at dispersing the populace—an ominous departure from the time-honored pattern of ritualized skirmishing. The campaign succeeded. Word that the Iroquois were seizing captives and torturing Jesuits shattered morale and prompted both Huron and French to abandon the country. Some of the surviving Hurons left with the Jesuits for the safety of Quebec. Others were adopted

Made from shell, wampum beads strung in standard lengths became units of currency in the European fur trade. The Indians valued wampum so highly that the Europeans eventually established a wampum factory on Long Island to satisfy the demand.

intact by Iroquois tribes, who themselves had lost many members recently to disease and readily assimilated their wards.

In their dealings with the Iroquois, the Dutch found that no item counted for more on the Indian scale of values than wampum—cylindrical beads that could be assembled into bracelets and belts, which were then exchanged by peoples of the region in solemn ceremonies such as the conclaves of the Iroquois League. Metal, cloth, and firearms all brought handsome returns from Indians at trading posts, but the ritual significance of wampum put it in a class by itself. The Dutch referred to wampum appreciatively as "the mother of the beaver trade," and its ap-

Delaware Indians negotiate trade agreements with Swedish colonists against a backdrop of a burial, a tribal battle, a family scene, and other aspects of native life depicted in this 17th-century sketch by Peter Lindestrom. The Swedish settlers were few in number, and their relations with the Indians were generally peaceful.

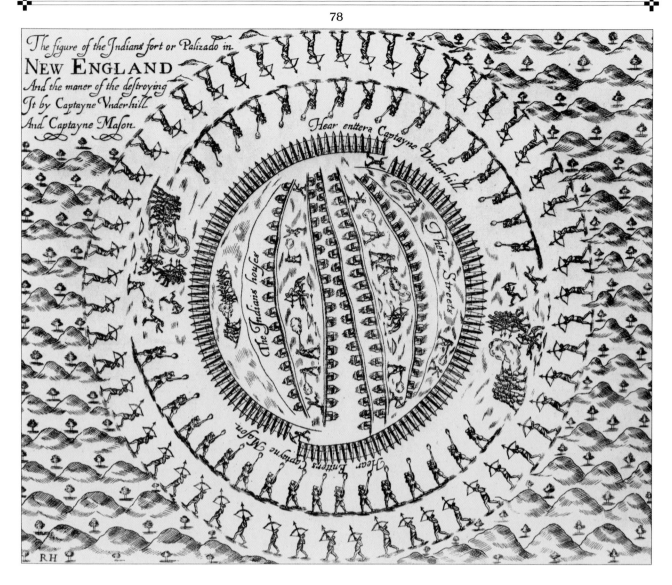

The figure of the Indians fort or Palizado in
NEW ENGLAND
And the maner of the destroying
It by Captayne Vnderhill
And Captayne Mason

Hear entters Captayne Vnderhill

The Indians houses

Their Streets

Hear Enters Captayne Mason

RH

peal was so broad that the Europeans themselves honored it as currency.

Wampum beads came in two forms: a white type made from whelk shells, and a purple variety fashioned from the quahog, a thick-shelled clam. The beads were painstakingly chipped, drilled, and polished—originally with stone tools and later with metal ones of European design—by coastal Indians such as the Algonquian-speaking Montauk of eastern Long Island. The villages of these wampum producers were the first stops for Dutch traders, who secured the beads for cloth and other Old World wares, carried the wampum up the Hudson and other inlets to fur-trading posts, and returned to Holland with pelts worth four or five times the value of the original cargo. Thus tribes hundreds of miles from prime fur country were exposed to the risks of European trade, including disease, dependency, and coercion by unscrupulous merchants, who eventually reduced some coastal Indians to virtual servitude by exacting prodigious amounts of wampum for clothing, tools, and other necessities that the people had at one time obtained for themselves.

A stylized engraving of the 1637 Pequot War by Captain John Underhill, an English soldier, shows an outer ring of Narragansett Indians and an inner ring of musket-bearing soldiers from the Connecticut and Massachusetts Bay colonies attacking a fortified Pequot village. Although the villagers are depicted as warriors, in truth most of them were old men, women, and children. Underhill has indicated where he and another officer entered the town and set it on fire.

The Dutch were not the only ones to profit as middlemen in the wampum trade. The assertive Pequot Indians of Connecticut collected wampum as tribute from coastal groups such as the Niantic and used the beads to trade with fur suppliers to their north and west. Their success raised concerns not only among their traditional rivals—notably the Narragansett of present-day Rhode Island—but also among Europeans. The Dutch, whose interests in Connecticut were limited to a few trading posts, sought to avoid conflict. But the strength of the Pequot incited the English, who not only coveted wampum and furs but sought land for settlers who were fanning out from the earliest English colonies along Massachusetts Bay.

Here, as in Virginia, English settlers were growing increasingly hostile to the Indians as their reliance on them for food and other help decreased. When the Protestant dissenters known as Pilgrims first came ashore at Plymouth in 1620, they had the good fortune to encounter Wampanoag Indians who were not only skilled farmers but kindly disposed to the English. One Indian named Squanto had visited England aboard a merchant ship and spoke the language well. Squanto became an intermediary for the Pilgrims with the Wampanoag sachem named Massasoit and taught the newcomers how to plant corn and to compost fish for fertilizer. Such native lessons, combined with European technology, soon brought the English success, and they began to extend their range. Before long, their desire for land and for profitable trade to defray the costs of colonization drew them into conflict with the Pequot.

The storm clouds began to gather in 1634, when Niantic Indians who were subject to the Pequot killed an English trader from Virginia named John Stone. The Massachusetts colonists demanded that the Pequot hand over the killers, pay a large indemnity in wampum, and allow them to purchase land in the Connecticut River valley for settlement. The Pequot agreed to the terms, asking only that the colonists send a trader who would deal with them directly. Two years later, that trader, John Oldham, was himself killed in his sloop when he clashed with Indians off the shores of Block Island. The people responsible for his death were subject to the Narragansett, rivals of the Pequot. But the English had already decided to entice the Narragansett into an alliance and so chose to blame the incident on the Pequot, insisting on a much larger wampum payment from that tribe, plus some of their children as hostages. Fighting soon broke out. When the Pequot killed nine English settlers and took two girls

The Wampanoag Indians of southeastern Massachusetts signed an oath of allegiance (right) to the Plymouth Colony in 1671. Both Christian names and phonetic equivalents of Indian names appear on the document; each of them is followed by a mark that served as a signature. The alliance soon dissolved over territorial disputes.

Metacomet (right), sachem of the Wampanoag of southeastern Massachusetts who was known to the English as King Philip, led an alliance of New England tribes in a bloody war against the 50,000 white settlers in the region between 1675 and 1676. The food bowl shown below, one carved from an elm burl, was found in his hut immediately after his death in battle.

prisoner, the Massachusetts Bay Colony and the recently formed Connecticut Colony declared an "offensive war."

Early on the morning of May 26, 1637, an army of 90 Englishmen and several hundred Indian allies—mainly Narragansett—descended on a fortified Pequot village along the Mystic River. Most of the able-bodied Pequot men were away. The English broke through the palisade and set fire to the wigwams. As many as 500 people either died in the flames or fled into the ranks of the waiting soldiers, where they were "received and entertained with the point of the sword," in the words of Captain John Underhill, who took part in the butchery. "Down fell men, women, and children," Underhill continued. "Those that escaped us fell into the hands of the Indians that were in the rear of us. Great and doleful was the bloody sight to the view of young soldiers who never had been in war, to see so many souls lie gasping on the ground, so thick, in some places, that you could hardly pass along." Underhill tried to justify the massacre by invoking a biblical precedent: "Should not Christians have more mercy and compassion? But I would refer you to David's war. When a people is grown to such a height of blood, and sin against God and man, and all confederates in the action, there he hath no respect to persons, but harrows them, and saws them, and puts them to the sword, and the most terriblest death that may be. We had sufficient light from the word of God for our proceedings."

In the months that followed, many more of the Pequot were killed, or shipped off to either Bermuda or the West Indies as slaves. The remainder were forced to submit to a treaty that dissolved them as an autonomous people. Soon, even the use of their name was outlawed—although proud descendants of the surviving Pequot would one day reassert their identity. As part of the spoils of war, the English garnered a small fortune in wampum.

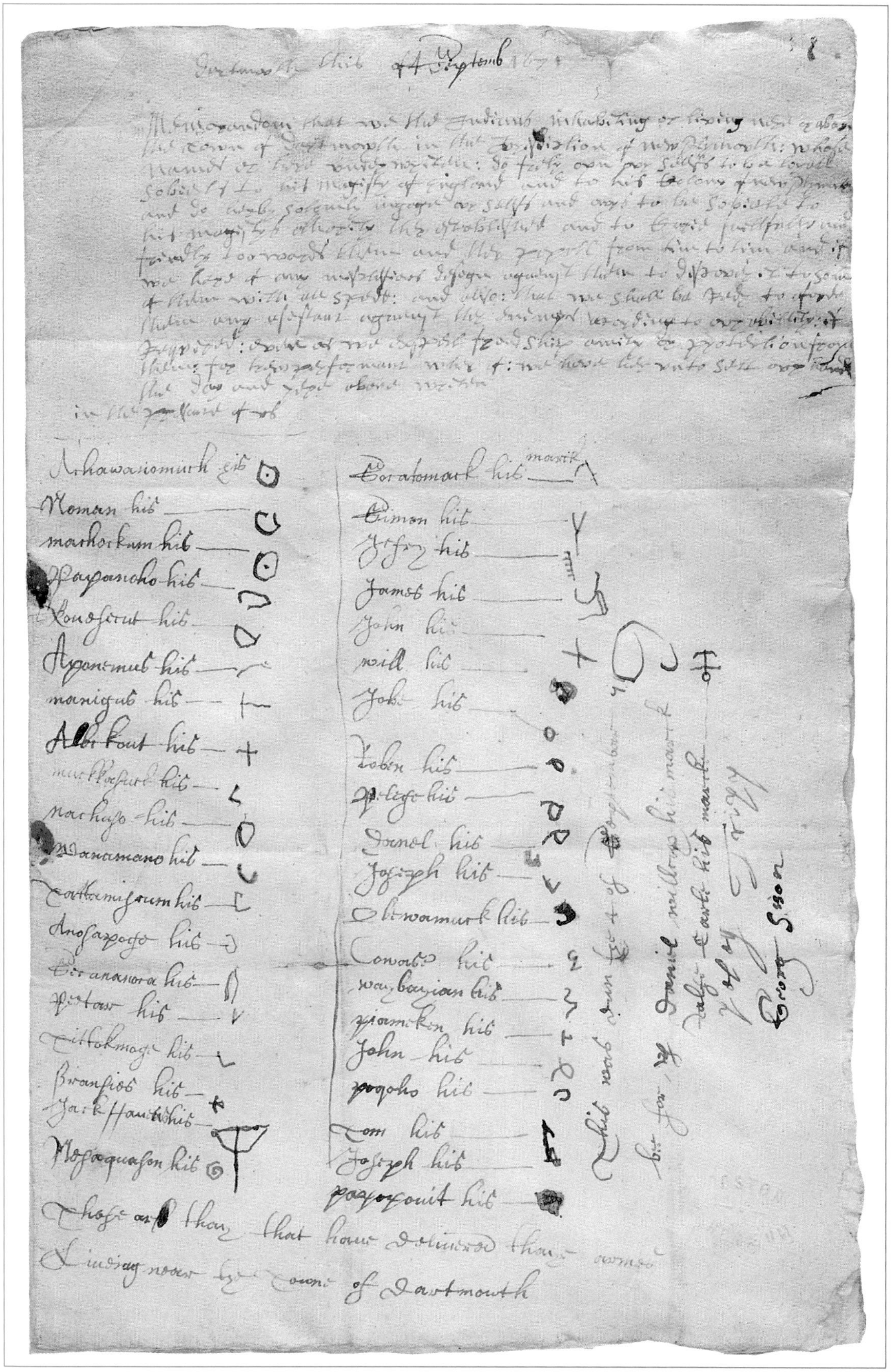

In the decades to come, English settlers extended their domain, filtering northward into New Hampshire and Vermont and pressing up against Dutch outposts along the Hudson. By the 1660s the Dutch found themselves outnumbered and outmaneuvered, and ceded their claims to the English, who then forged a compact of convenience with the powerful Iroquois. Meanwhile, several New England tribes that had cooperated earlier with the English discovered that their goodwill had earned them no respite from the colonists' territorial demands. Like other devout Europeans who came to the New World, the settlers of New England saw themselves as instruments of Providence, divinely appointed to claim the New World from its "godless" peoples. John Winthrop, son of Connecticut's governor, insisted that the terrible diseases ravaging local tribes—including groups loyal to the early settlers—were God's way of clearing "our title to this place." If God was working to dispossess the Indians, colonists felt justified in brushing aside the survivors.

Ultimately, land-hungry English settlers alienated the very people who had befriended the Pilgrims at Plymouth. When leadership of the Wampanoag passed to Massasoit's son Metacomet in 1662, the sachem inherited a dwindling domain. Here, as elsewhere in the Northeast, settlers were eating away at tribal territory through dubious purchases of land. In some cases, Indians entered into deals without fully understanding the terms, or bartered land claimed by another tribe. Increasingly, whites were exploiting Indian dependence on trade goods to gain concessions. Particularly galling to Metacomet was the English practice of plying his people with liquor, then making them pay for it by signing away land. Finally, the frustrated sachem—known to the English as King Philip—tried to coax other tribes of the region into a confederation to resist such encroachments. In 1675 a Christianized Indian told English authorities at Plymouth that Philip, whose people had obtained firearms through trade, was preparing for war. This informer was

Indians who fought on the side of the English in King Philip's War, many of them converted Christians, were awarded brass "peace" medals by the colonists. The English benefited greatly from Indian assistance; a Native American ally is reported to have fired the shot that killed King Philip.

murdered shortly thereafter, and three Indians close to Philip were tried and hanged for the deed, bringing tensions to the flash point.

Fighting first broke out around Plymouth in June and quickly spread across the countryside. When colonists learned that some of the Wampanoag had fled to the Narragansett—former allies of the English in the Pequot War—they insisted that the refugees, mostly women and children, be handed over. The Narragansett sachem Canonchet, who was sympathetic to Philip and knew that the Wampanoag would probably be sold into slavery, flatly refused. "No," he said when pressed for the fugitives, "not a Wampanoag, nor the paring of a Wampanoag's nail." Late that fall, an army of 1,000 colonists marched against the Narragansett, attacking one of their villages in Rhode Island and killing as many as 300 warriors and 300 women and children. In the aftermath, Canonchet launched raids against English settlements, but he was soon tracked down with the help of Indians loyal to the English, and executed.

Philip, for his part, led his own warriors westward in the depths of winter to seek allies among a conclave of Algonquian Indians gathered near Albany. But his hopes were dashed when the Mohawk attacked the assembled forces at the urging of New York's governor and drove Philip and his insurgents back to Massachusetts. Claiming that they now faced a grand conspiracy, colonists lashed out at Indians throughout New England, burning villages and meeting Indian outbursts with crushing reprisals. By the summer of 1676, the uprising had been stamped out. That August, Philip and his few remaining followers were trapped and killed in a swamp on the old Wampanoag lands.

King Philip's War had wreaked havoc, costing the English some 600 lives. The Indians, already weakened by diseases and the disruption of their culture, had lost 3,000 men, women, and children. In New England, their last hope of halting European expansion was gone. Elsewhere in the Northeast, it was just a matter of time.

As King Philip lay dead, the commander of the attacking force, Captain Benjamin Church, sought out his body, curious to see what manner of man he had been fighting. His response spoke volumes about the age—and echoed something that had happened nearly two centuries earlier. Like the mariners who had spotted running figures in the distance as they sailed with John Cabot along a northern coast in 1497, this English soldier was not sure he saw a man at all. King Philip, he said, looked like "a doleful, great, naked, dirty beast." He ordered the body quartered and decapitated, and took the head away with him as a trophy. ✦

A GREENLAND TRAGEDY

No one knows the exact fate of the Viking settlers who were the first Europeans to reach Greenland. But the oral history of the local Eskimo peoples offers at least one chilling explanation.

The story was committed to paper by an Eskimo named Aron of Kangek during the late 1850s. After having been confined to his bed by tuberculosis, Aron spent the final years of his life recording the ancient legends of his people and illustrating them with watercolor paintings.

Aron's ancestors had migrated to Greenland from their homeland in Alaska sometime around the year 880, about a century before the arrival of the Viking outlaw Erik the Red and his followers. According to Eskimo tradition, the initial encounters between these two seafaring peoples of different races were friendly. But the peaceful coexistence swiftly degenerated into bloody confrontations. It was one of these clashes, illustrated here in Aron's watercolors, that brought the European presence to a violent end.

As related in the legend, the trouble began when the Norsemen hired an Eskimo servant girl by the name of Navaranak. No sooner had Navaranak mastered the Norse language than she started to spread false rumors among her employers that the Eskimos were growing resentful of them. At the same time, "this shameful woman," as Aron described her, succeeded in alarming her own people with dire predictions of Viking aggression.

A tragedy grew out of this climate of fear and misunderstanding. Under the mistaken impression that the Eskimos were secretly planning to attack them, the Vikings staged a preemptive raid against an unprotected Eskimo village. The Eskimos promptly retaliated by completely wiping out the intruders' settlement. And from that time forward, in the words of chronicler Aron, "there were no longer any Norsemen in any of the fjords."

85

Eskimo seal hunters
in a kayak and in a
larger boat called
an umiak discover a
Norse settlement at
the head of an inlet.
"They saw a very
large house," wrote
the 19th-century
chronicler Aron.
"But as yet, there
were no people to
be seen." Undetect-
ed, the hunters pad-
dled back to their
village to tell the
other Eskimos of
the newcomers.

Led by the seal-hunting crew, a group of Eskimo men, women, and children pay a call
on the Norse village and receive a warm
welcome. This first delegation was followed
by many more. The Norsemen and the Eskimos subsequently learned to understand
one another's language and "there were the
most friendly relations between them."

The amity between Viking and Eskimo is brutally shattered when a band of spear-wielding Vikings storms an Eskimo village. At the time of the attack, the men of the village were away hunting caribou.

Two Norsemen hold aloft the severed head of an Eskimo mother. Her corpse and that of her slain newborn lie at the Vikings' feet. Another woman cowered nearby in a rock crevice, a hidden witness to the grisly scene.

With the Norsemen gone, the woman who escaped the massacre examines the bodies of the dead. When the hunters returned, Aron wrote, "the husband of the killed woman with the baby was beside himself with grief and rage." He sought out a skilled shaman to help the Eskimos plot their revenge against the Vikings.

The Eskimos build an umiak and cover it with bleached skins. When the vessel was finished, reported Aron, "it looked like a piece of dirty ice without a trace of human life, although it was crammed full of people inside, who could see everything that happened through numerous small holes bored here and there in the sides."

As the Eskimos drift toward the Viking village in their camouflaged boat, one of the Norsemen shades his eyes, peers at the horizon, and shouts the alarm: "Here come the Eskimos!" But his companions jeered: "That is no boat; it is merely some ice floes."

Seemingly secure inside their house of stone, the Vikings entertain themselves by twirling a stick with the decapitated woman's head impaled on one end. Meanwhile outside, the shaman was casting a spell designed to keep the Norsemen unaware of the presence of the attacking Eskimos, who were building a fire of brushwood around the entrance to the house.

Having set fire to the dwelling, the Eskimos block the Vikings' path of escape. Most of the Norsemen perished in the conflagration, and those who slipped through the flames were shot full of arrows. Only one made good his escape: the Norse leader Ungortok, who took his infant son in his arms and sprang out of a window "with a tremendous leap."

Slowed by the weight of his son, Ungortok steadily loses ground to the Eskimos (above, right). In desperation, the Viking chief saves himself by tossing the child into a lake and leaving him to drown. "Bitterness added wings to his flight," wrote Aron, "so that it was as though he was blown along from behind by his pursuers." He then escapes by sea (above), imploring a spirit to "send me now your strong morning breeze." The Viking ship sped off so swiftly that the Eskimos could not overtake it.

With the Norsemen gone, the Eskimos turned their wrath on the cause of the tragedy, the servant girl Navaranak, binding her hands and topknot with sealskin straps and dragging her over the ground. "They punished her to death in this manner," Aron wrote, "because she had destroyed the friendship of Greenlanders and Norsemen."

Near the ruins of Pecos Pueblo stand the sun-gilded remains of a Spanish church and the low circular wall marking a kiva, an Indian underground ceremonial chamber. The two structures are mute reminders of an uneasy coexistence between missionary aspirations and Native American beliefs.

A CITY SIGHTLY AND STRONG

As the conquistadors made their way north from Mexico at the beginning of the 16th century, they encountered communities of agricultural people living in huge multistory, interconnected dwellings. The Spaniards called the settlements, and by extension the Indians who lived in them, pueblos, after their own word for village. The eastern frontier of the Pueblo Indian domain lay at the foot of the Sangre de Cristo mountain range at the southern tip of the Rockies. There, on a small mesa about 25 miles southeast of present-day Santa Fe, stood a fortress pueblo described by one of the first Spaniards to see it as "a city sightly and strong." Known as Pekush to neighboring peoples, it became Pecos to the invaders. Pecos guarded the entrance to the Glorieta Pass, a four-mile-long, east-west passage through the Sangre de Cristo foothills from the Rio Grande Valley to the edge of the Great Plains. As gatekeeper to this strategic corridor, the pueblo stood at a cultural and commercial crossroads of the Indian, and later the Spanish, world.

PECOS AT
ITS HEIGHT

A wooden ladder provides access to this reconstructed kiva through the opening that served as both entryway and chimney. A stone deflector placed beside the firepit shielded the flame from drafts.

"It is feared throughout the land," wrote the Spaniard Pedro de Castañeda of Pecos Pueblo in 1540, when the Spaniards first visited there. The pueblo, then at the peak of its power and influence, housed 2,000 inhabitants in airy four- to five-story terraced apartments built around a large central courtyard. The entire complex covered about four acres. The rocky mesa on which the pueblo stood provided a natural defensive position. The city's 500 warriors had a commanding view of the surrounding countryside from the tiers of walkways that rimmed the structure. Below the mesa, in the rich alluvial bottom lands of the Pecos River, crops of corn, beans, and squash grew in abundance.

Fashioned from the abundant clay in the hills around the pueblo, a tiny human effigy only 2.5 inches high and a miniature vessel probably served as ceremonial objects. The Pecos Indians were skilled and prolific potters.

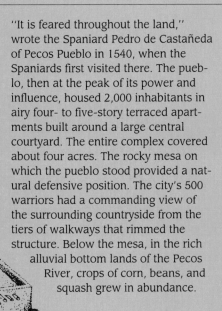

The windowless ground-floor rooms of the pueblo served as food storage chambers. The living quarters located above, which housed extended families, were connected by lightweight ladders that could be quickly pulled up by hand in the event of conflict.

THE GREAT TRADE FAIR

Pecos Pueblo's location along the narrow pass through the mountains gave it preeminence in the thriving commerce between the farmers of the upper Rio Grande Valley and the nomads of the Great Plains. The city's principal trading partners were the Apache, who for most of the year followed the buffalo herds. But at harvesttime, they came west by the hundreds to Pecos, bringing trains of dogs pulling travois that were loaded with meat, hides, and tallow to exchange for the crops, textiles, and pottery produced by the pueblos.

A modern painting of the harvesttime trade fair at Pecos shows pueblo residents descending to the Apache encampment in the field below their city walls, carrying squash, corn, cotton clothing, and pottery—their staple items of trade. Shells, chipped stone knives, and birds such as the caged eagle pictured here were also bartered at these meetings.

A 15th-century clay pot known as an olla is typical of the thickly glazed, richly colored red and brown ware that was made by pueblo artisans and traded during that period.

THE INFLUENCE OF THE FRIARS

Starting with the arrival of the first Spanish settlers in New Mexico in 1598, a succession of Franciscan friars took up residence in Pecos seeking to use the pueblo as a base for missionary activities there and in the Great Plains. By 1625 they had constructed a large church and *convento,* or parish hall, at the south end of the mesa, a few feet from the walls of the pueblo.

The friars, one of them wrote, built the church "with room for all the people of the pueblo." Although members of the community attended services in the church, most of them also continued to practice their own religion, worshiping in their kivas and politely rejecting the friars' concept of a single church and lone deity.

Decorated with a traditional Pecos motif thought to be a feathered serpent, this bowl dating from the pueblo's mission years subtly attests to the persistence of native culture under Spanish rule.

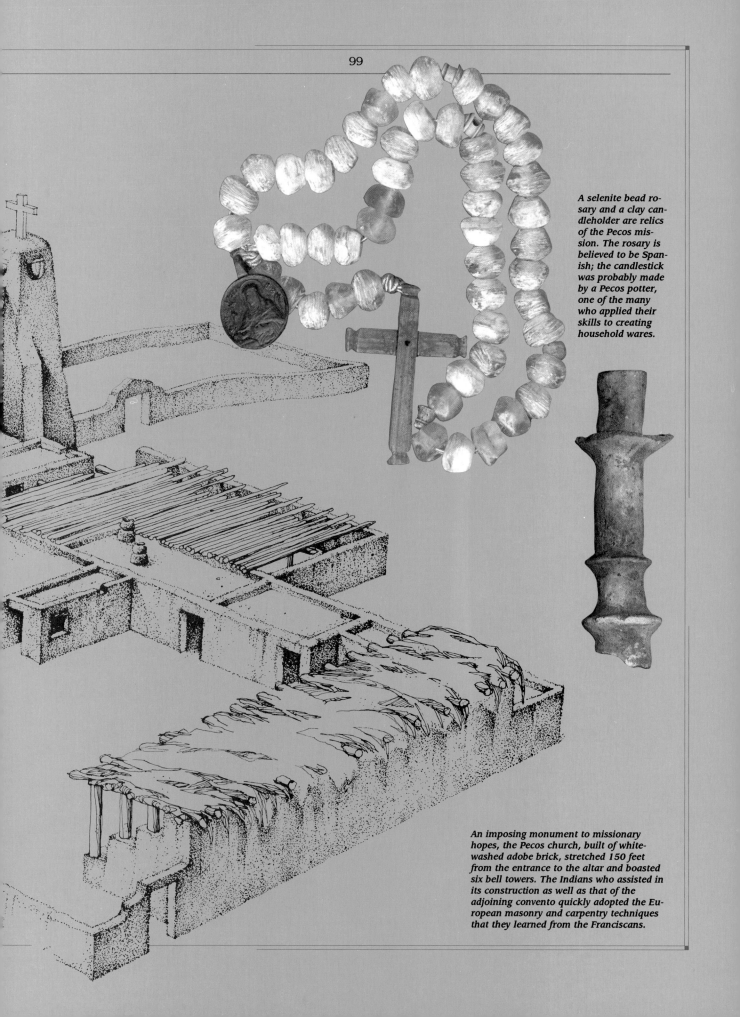

A selenite bead rosary and a clay candleholder are relics of the Pecos mission. The rosary is believed to be Spanish; the candlestick was probably made by a Pecos potter, one of the many who applied their skills to creating household wares.

An imposing monument to missionary hopes, the Pecos church, built of whitewashed adobe brick, stretched 150 feet from the entrance to the altar and boasted six bell towers. The Indians who assisted in its construction as well as that of the adjoining convento quickly adopted the European masonry and carpentry techniques that they learned from the Franciscans.

THE DOWNFALL OF AN INDIAN COMMUNITY

In 1680 Pecos rose against its foreign occupiers, joining other pueblos in a united revolt that briefly drove the Spaniards out of present-day New Mexico. The Indians razed the mission church and for a time lived again as their ancestors had. But the seeds of the pueblo's demise had already taken root. A small group of converted Christians remained loyal to the Spaniards, creating a deep rift in the community even before the Spaniards returned 12 years after the revolt. Throughout the mid-1700s, Comanche raiders repeatedly attacked border pueblos, forcing the farmers of Pecos to abandon their fertile bottom lands. A succession of smallpox epidemics ravaged the population. By century's end, about 30 families lived inside the walls of the dying pueblo, and in 1838, just 17 people remained. That year, they left Pecos, moving 80 miles west to Jemez Pueblo, where their descendants live today.

Ravaged by weather and vandals, the shell of a second Pecos church, completed in 1717, rests atop the foundation walls of the original mission.

Wahu Toya, photographed in 1880 as an old man, left Pecos in the 1838 emigration to Jemez and thus was among the last group of Pecos Indians to live in their ancient home.

3

THE PLIGHT OF THE PUEBLOS

Painted on buffalo hide by a Native American artist of the Southwest around 1675, this image of the Virgin Mary is endowed with Indian features. The Pueblo Indians drew parallels between Christianity and their own spiritual traditions, such as likening the Blessed Mother to their female deity Iakitu who was revered as a universal grandmother and the giver of corn.

Word of the invaders had preceded them, and some 700 Zuni of Hawikuh Pueblo prepared to defend their homes. The women and children were sent to safety, while swift runners dashed to friendly pueblos with appeals for reinforcements. By the time the strangers finally appeared before the town on a tributary of the river later known as the Colorado, perhaps 200 warriors stood ready for battle. Others remained inside the adobe walls to fight among the narrow passageways should the intruders break through.

The strangers who approached that fateful morning were like no people the Zuni had encountered. There were about 100 of them, pale complexioned and bearded, encased from waist to neck in a turtlelike shell of glittering metal; another carapace protected their heads. The strangers carried formidable spears and long, gleaming metal knives. The Indians had heard vaguely of another weapon: a heavy stick that flashed fire and thunder, and brought death at great distances. More awesome still, many of the white warriors traveled astride what a Zuni scout had described as "fierce, man-eating animals"—beasts so huge and swift that the earth trembled beneath their hoofs.

The foremost of the assembled warriors, armed with clubs and bows and arrows, and carrying leather shields, sprinkled a line of sacred corn-meal along the ground, forbidding the outlanders to cross. When the strangers shouted commands in an unintelligible tongue and lowered their weapons, the Indians responded with a shower of arrows. The white men surged forward, howling their battle cry.

The struggle for Hawikuh lasted less than an hour. After killing perhaps a dozen of the Indians, the terrifying strangers were content to cease their attack and stood aside while the Zuni filed dazedly from their pueblo. Then, the white men helped themselves to Hawikuh's domesticated turkeys and storerooms full of maize and beans.

So began two centuries and more of unequal struggle that would devastate the pueblos and forever alter the lives of the Zuni, indeed of every Indian man, woman, and child in the American Southwest.

The date was July 7, 1540, and the conquerors of Hawikuh were Spaniards under the command of Francisco Vásquez de Coronado, a provincial governor in the vast and immensely rich dependency of New Spain. Scarcely half a century had passed since Columbus first set foot on the shores of the Americas. Yet in that brief time, conquistadors had added a sizable portion of the Western Hemisphere to the Spanish Crown. Francisco Pizarro and Hernán Cortés, each leading a mere handful of men, had destroyed the Inca Empire of Peru and dismantled the Aztec kingdom

A rock painting in a cave in Sonora, Mexico, dating from the 1530s, probably depicts one Indian's fleeting glimpse of an early Spanish explorer wearing a plumed helmet and perhaps riding north to New Mexico. The pictographs on the caves and cliffs of the Southwest are the only records of Native Americans' impressions of the white invaders.

of Mexico. The wealth of gold, silver, and gemstones that flowed through the royal counting house at Seville was indescribable. And there was reason to believe that more lay to the north beyond the Rio Grande.

The earliest explorers of this land were galvanized by tales of fabulous cities where the streets were paved with gold and the inhabitants draped with jewels. The stories evoked a legend reaching back to the eighth century when the Moors of North Africa invaded Spain and Portugal, bringing Islam to the Iberian Peninsula. The legend told of seven Catholic bishops who fled the infidels by sailing westward to the beautiful island of Antilia where each bishop founded a utopian community filled with riches. Spanish navigators had failed to locate a trace of these seven cities of gold, but the myth refused to die. In the summer of 1536, it received new life when four survivors of Pánfilo de Narváez's lost expedition to the west coast of Florida miraculously turned up in Mexico City, capital of New Spain. Missing for more than eight years, the men—Narváez's treasurer Álvar Núñez Cabeza de Vaca, two other Spanish officers, and a black slave known as Esteban the Moor—had trekked across northern Mexico after being shipwrecked on the coast of present-day Texas. During their wanderings, a tribe in the Sonora Valley had told them of a land to the north where a people of great wealth dwelled.

This scrap of information inspired the viceroy of New Spain, Antonio de Mendoza, to investigate. In 1539 Mendoza sent Marcos de Niza, a renowned Franciscan friar and explorer, accompanied by Esteban, up the west coast of Mexico and through the desert of present-day Arizona. Ranging ahead of the main party, Esteban reached Hawikuh where the Zuni at first welcomed him, but then for reasons lost to history—perhaps because they considered him a sorcerer—suddenly attacked and killed him. Several of the Moor's Indian retainers escaped to warn the friar, who called off the search, but not before he had pushed on to a hilltop where he could see Hawikuh on the hazy horizon. The friar's rich imagination greatly enhanced the image. Hawikuh, Fray Marcos later reported, was "bigger than the city of Mexico." Friendly Indians had told him that it was the smallest of seven cities "under one lord" in a region known as Cíbola, where "women wore strings of gold beads and men girdles of gold."

That was why, a year later, Coronado with Fray Marcos as guide led an expedition into the land now known as New Mexico on a mission of "Glory, God, and Gold." As it turned out, Fray Marcos was much mistaken. There was no gold. Yet hope dies hard, and in the meantime, there was a vast new land and perhaps other wealth for a conquistador to claim for Spain and self, new souls for the padres to save, and glory enough for most men in the service of God and king.

What followed would reflect a certain credit on Spanish intentions, if not deeds. Abiding by royal decree and the design of the Catholic Church, Viceroy Mendoza would insist that the conquest be "apostolic and Christian, and not butchery." The Indians were to be converted and civilized— ideals that soon foundered on the harsh realities of frontier life.

The settled, agricultural Pueblo peoples would not yield easily to the superior arms of the Europeans. From time to time, the Indians would rise up and strike their oppressors, and at one point would drive every last Spaniard from New Mexico. But the conquistadors would return and, in the end, subjugate the Indians. Although drought and disease, slaughter, and exploitation reduced the pueblos to a mere remnant of the thriving society that existed before Coronado, the surviving Indians clung stubbornly to their ancient traditions and age-old beliefs.

Coronado had come north to Hawikuh with only an advance guard. He sent word for the main body of his expedition—more than 200 Spanish men-at-arms along with hundreds of Indian auxiliaries, black servants, and herdsmen for the pack animals, cattle, sheep, and swine—to join him at Hawikuh. After seizing the village, he attempted to make amends with the Zuni. Through his Indian allies, he assured the Indians hiding in the

Towering above the New Mexico desert, the sacred Corn Mountain, or "Towaya'llone," was a refuge for hundreds of Zunis following the seizure of their pueblo—and reserve store of food—by Francisco Vásquez de Coronado's men in the battle of Hawikuh.

Zuni warriors with shields defend Hawikuh Pueblo against the Spaniards, as imagined in this allegorical drawing by a Christianized Mexican Indian living in the 16th century. The sketch illustrates the ambition of the invaders—who are armed with Bibles, rosaries, and crucifixes—to convert what they perceived to be heathen Indians.

mountains that no harm would come to them if they returned to Hawikuh. The Zuni may have felt that they had no option. In any case, a delegation soon appeared. Coronado greeted them, and after some urging, they agreed to return and embrace Christianity.

The Franciscan friars busied themselves with baptisms, and for the moment, all was apostolic, as the viceroy wished. In a letter to his superior, Coronado related that he had found no evidence of the great urban complex and vast mineral wealth reported by Fray Marcos, whom he had sent back to Mexico in disgrace. The friar, he wrote, "has not told the truth in a single thing he has said, except the name of the cities and the large stone houses." But Coronado was not discouraged. He would press on "throughout all the surrounding regions in order to find out if there is anything worthwhile."

The Spaniards would have been astounded at the speed with which news of the conquest of Hawikuh traveled to the farthest reaches of the Pueblo lands. Compared to the Aztec and Inca empires, it was a small, circumscribed world, containing perhaps 60,000 people. In addition to a few thousand Zunis along the Zuni River, a like number of Hopis inhabited seven pueblos near four precipitous mesas 100 miles to the west in what is today northeastern Arizona. The bulk of the Pueblo population comprised two broad language groups—Tanoan and Keresan—and lived in more than 100 pueblos clustered around the Rio Grande and its tributaries in New Mexico. Although closely allied in appearance and culture, these Indians spoke in distinct tongues. So diverse were the dialects that people in pueblos a few miles apart might not be able to converse readily. Moreover, feuds and rivalries so dominated their lives that even likespeaking Indians sometimes found themselves at odds. This lack of cohesion would work both for and against the Spaniards. It made conquering the pueblos easier, but controlling them more difficult.

The Spaniards, of course, knew none of this beforehand. But soon they were offered some new information about the lands they were seeking to subdue. A delegation of Indians from Pecos, 200 miles to the east, appeared at Hawikuh, possibly seeking to appease the fearsome new gods or perhaps simply to fulfill their curiosity. The principal ambassador was a tall young man whom Coronado dubbed Bigotes, or "whiskers"; an older companion the Spaniards called Cacique, or "governor." The Indians invited Coronado to their country. They said they knew nothing of gold or silver, but that their homeland was rich in food and turquoise and was the gateway to the plains where roamed vast herds of buffalo—whose tanned hides Coronado had already admired among the Zuni.

Bigotes and Cacique offered themselves to the Spaniards as guides, and Coronado immediately dispatched Captain Hernando de Alvarado with 20 soldiers and a friar to explore eastward. Alvarado set forth on August 29. In the ensuing weeks, he and his company traveled 700 miles through a land that no white man had seen before; they visited or observed no fewer than 80 pueblos and found friendship and hospitality everywhere; Indians showered them with gifts and accepted symbols of the Christian God and Spanish Crown. Many crosses were erected and baptisms performed. So felicitous was the reception that Alvarado sent word to Coronado that he should establish a winter camp at Tiguex, a province of 12 pueblos lining both sides of the Rio Grande near where Albuquerque stands today. The

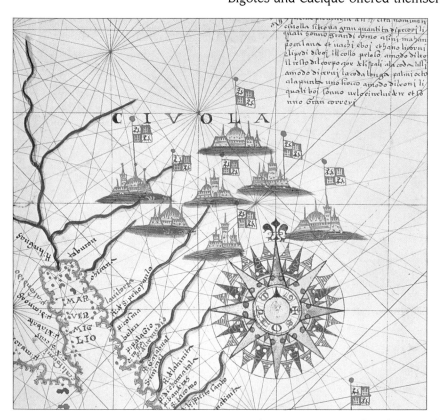

A detail from a 16th-century map depicts the Seven Cities of Cíbola, reputed to be rich in jewels and gold, that Coronado and others hoped to find in the American Southwest. The myth of Cíbola conformed with contemporary reports of wealthy Indian cultures flourishing north of Mexico.

captain went on to see the plains and the limitless herds of buffalo, which he described as living in "such multitudes that I do not know what to compare them with unless it be the fish in the sea."

At Pecos, Alvarado met the Indian the Spaniards would call El Turco. A Pawnee captive, whose dark visage resembled that of a Turk, the man quickly understood what gold and silver meant to a conquistador and concocted a plan to lure the Spaniards north, whence he might escape to his homeland. Using sign language, El Turco spun a tale of a fabulous land called Quivira that was wealthy beyond belief. He himself, said the Pawnee, had owned a gold bracelet from Quivira, but the Pecos chiefs, Bigotes and Cacique, had taken it from him. Fired with visions of treasure, Alvarado confronted his hosts in Pecos. When Bigotes and Cacique loudly denied knowledge of such a bracelet, Alvarado put them in chains and hauled them west to Tiguex, where he would wait for Coronado.

Meanwhile, at Tiguex, the Spaniards were making other mistakes. Encouraged by Alvarado's report, Coronado had sent another captain, García López de Cárdenas, to prepare winter quarters for the advance guard and the main body still struggling north from Mexico. At first, López de Cárdenas planned an encampment outside pueblo walls. But it was late fall by now, and the soldiers were suffering in the biting wind and cold. López de Cárdenas asked that the Indians turn over one of their Tiguex pueblos. The inhabitants of Alcanfor vacated their homes and scattered to find shelter among kinsmen.

Shortly afterward, Coronado arrived and demanded hundreds of cotton and animal-skin cloaks for his men. When his hosts protested, he sent soldiers to seize the garments, some going so far as to strip them

Remote mesa-top villages such as Walpi Pueblo in Hopi territory were imposing obstacles for hostile Spanish forces. Walpi Pueblo was established in the 1680s after the Hopi joined other pueblos in a revolt against the Spanish and left their low-lying villages to seek safety on the heights.

from the backs of the pueblo dwellers. The Indians retaliated by raiding the Spanish corrals, slaughtering a number of horses and mules. In a fury, Coronado ordered López de Cárdenas to destroy the nearby pueblos of Arenal and Moho. At Arenal, the Spaniards killed some 200 Indians, burning many of them at the stake to the pitiful wails of their women and children.

It was now early January, and the remainder of Coronado's force had arrived. Even so, it took a winter-long siege before the defenders of Moho gave up. In the end, it was a lack of water, not Spanish arms, that undid them. There was only one inadequate well, and after the winter snows disappeared in March, the Indians began to suffer from thirst. They first surrendered 100 of their women and children. A fortnight later, the warriors and the remaining women and children attempted to slip away. An alert sentry shouted an alarm. Spanish horsemen

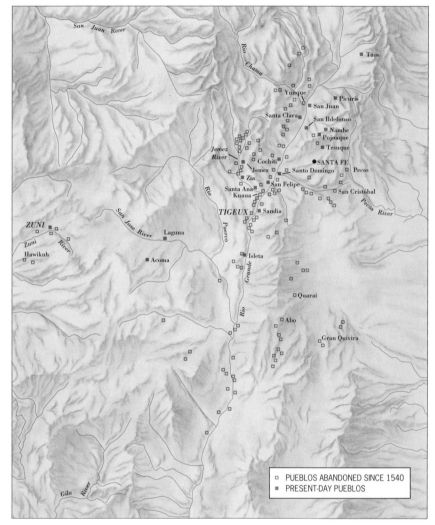

charged, thrusting and slashing with lances and swords. In their efforts to escape, some of the Indians threw themselves into the icy Rio Grande, where many perished. The Spaniards made slaves of the survivors.

By early April, all of Tiguex had fled to the mountains, and Coronado could again wrap himself in the vision of riches. He had, of course, summoned El Turco immediately upon his arrival, and the Pawnee again painted a glittering picture of Quivira. "There was so much gold," a chronicler reported, "that they could load not only horses but wagons with it." In this place, even the common folk quaffed from golden bowls; the king traveled in a huge canoe with golden oarlocks, and he reclined beneath a tree hung with little gold bells, whose soft tinkling lulled him to

When Coronado entered New Mexico in 1540, there were more than 100 thriving pueblos along the Rio Grande and its tributaries. In the ensuing centuries, most of these Indian villages were abandoned for a number of reasons—drought, famine, intertribal warfare, and the edicts of the Spanish colonial authorities. Today, only a handful of the original pueblos remain inhabited.

sleep. El Turco repeated the story of the golden bracelet. When Bigotes and Cacique again denied all knowledge, Coronado set attack dogs on them. Though badly mauled, the two could not be made to confess. No matter. Coronado would see for himself come spring.

His army departed Tiguex on April 23, 1541. In the pueblos they passed, the terrified inhabitants remained behind barricades—except in Pecos where there was wild rejoicing at the sight of Bigotes and Cacique, long since given up for dead. Magnanimously, Coronado released the two sorely used chiefs. For five weeks, the expedition moved 600 miles through what is now eastern New Mexico and the Texas Panhandle, admiring the expanse of grass and buffalo but finding no great cities or precious metals. After resting, Coronado took three dozen men and with El Turco struck out northward, across present-day Oklahoma and Kansas. Eleven days later, he came upon the first settlement, a cluster of grass huts

This Spanish woodcut of an American bison, based on descriptions from explorers of the Southwest during the 16th century, is possibly the first view Europeans had of the animal that was so essential to Native American life.

located downriver from the great bend of the Arkansas River. For 25 days, the party explored Quivira. "There is not any gold, nor any other metal—nothing but little villages," Coronado reported.

The frustrated Spaniards turned on El Turco, torturing him until he confessed to his lies. They swiftly garroted him and turned back for another bitter winter spent within the province of Tiguex. In the spring of 1542, two and a half years after starting north with such dazzling hopes, Coronado gave up. He freed all the Indians he had enslaved and led the tattered remnant of his expedition—scarcely 100 of the original 300 men—home to Mexico. Coronado died obscure and broken in Mexico City 12 years later. Only the Franciscan friars had found treasure. Three of them remained behind to convert the pueblo dwellers. All three soon experienced a martyr's death, and for the next 40 years, the Indians resumed the lives they had lived before the coming of the white men.

Coronado's departure did not restore complete tranquillity to the region, where life had long been fraught with hazards. As an agricultural people, the pueblo dwellers depended heavily on the weather. A lack of rain could bring famine, forcing a community to relocate. There was also the constant problem of maintaining peace. Although war, in the sense of large battles, was unknown, raids and skirmishes did occur. Hostilities might erupt due to competition for scarce food supplies or farmland. Another possible source of conflict was the never-ending suspicion of witchcraft or evil spirits invoked by individuals. This strife was complicated by the threat posed by bands of Plains Indians.

The Plains Apache, nomadic hunter-gatherers, began arriving in the area from the east during the late 1500s and early 1600s. A few pueblos, notably Pecos and Taos, became trading centers where the Apache and other Plains tribes exchanged their dried meat, wild plants, and buffalo skins for turkeys, crops, blankets, baskets, and finely crafted pueblo tools. But these vigorous people were also prone to plunder. Raiding pueblos became a cornerstone of Apache and, later, Navajo culture. Also, in the last years of the 16th century, the Spaniards started north again, bent on establishing another frontier province for New Spain.

The colony would be called New Mexico, and to command the venture, the Crown had chosen a man of wealth and position: Don Juan de Oñate, scion of a renowned silver mining family, who had successfully developed mines and pacified Indians in Mexico. His wife was a grand-

The ancestors of this group of Zuni elders, shown in a photograph that was taken in 1879 at their pueblo in New Mexico, were the first Native American inhabitants of the Southwest to resist the Spanish onslaught.

daughter of Cortés as well as a great-granddaughter of the Aztec emperor Montezuma.

A few parties of Spaniards, mainly on prospecting expeditions, had entered the pueblo country in the last two decades of the century. But they were nothing like Oñate's cavalcade of colonists, soldiers, priests, and Indian retainers that crossed the Rio Grande near present-day El Paso on April 30, 1598. Memories of Coronado's army remained strong there, and pueblo after pueblo lay deserted at Oñate's approach. On July 7, in the kiva of the town the Spaniards had named Santo Domingo, he convened a gathering of seven Indian leaders said to represent 33 pueblos. Through translators, Oñate announced that he had been sent by the greatest king in all the world, Philip II of Spain, to gather the Indians into his arms and save their souls so that they could live forever in justice, prosperity, and peace. He described the obligation of subjects to obey laws and orders, and warned that transgressors would be severely punished. Then, Oñate portrayed the joys of Christianity: life after death and eternal bliss in the presence of God; otherwise, their fate would be hell's fire and perpetual torment. Much of this surely was lost in translation, first from Castilian into Mexican Indian, then into Pueblo tongues. Even if it were perfectly transmitted, the concept of heaven, hell, a distant pope, and one God would have been incomprehensible to a people who worshiped a multiplicity of deities and had no conception of a supreme ruler. Ultimate power in each pueblo had always rested with a council of elders, and the peoples' lives centered on maintaining harmony within the community, and between the community and the world of plants and animals. Perhaps what the Indians did understand was the efficiency of Spanish weapons. When Oñate issued his demands, they quickly pledged their fealty.

Three days after leaving Santo Domingo, Oñate and his horsemen arrived at the pueblo of Okhe, soon to be known as San Juan Pueblo, on the east bank of the Rio Grande about 30 miles north of the future Santa Fe. The land rolled away from the river in beautiful hills and mesas, and fields of maize, beans, and squash lay ripening in the summer sun. Such prospects were heartening to the colonists, for they would depend on the Indians for much of their food. At first, it was willingly given and scrupulously paid for. But as demands piled up, the Indians grew less eager to part with their reserves. Now, another issue arose: Where would the Spaniards find shelter from the harsh New Mexican winter?

When the main expedition arrived one month later, the Spaniards took over the pueblo of Yunque, at the confluence of the Rio Grande and Rio Chama. They renamed it San Gabriel and, in thanks for their good fortune, erected the first Christian church in the Southwest. Meanwhile, soldiers scoured the countryside requisitioning food, skins, blankets, and firewood to carry the colonists through the winter.

The explosion came late in the year at the pueblo of Acoma atop a 357-foot mesa 140 miles southwest of San Gabriel. Anxiously seeking the mineral wealth that would justify the colony, Oñate with 100 men had struck out on an expedition into Arizona. And now his nephew Juan de Zaldívar led another 30 men to join Oñate. By the time he reached Acoma on December 1, Zaldívar was in need of provisions. He was willing to trade, but the Indians had already supplied Oñate, and their storerooms were growing empty. When Zaldívar insisted, they made a show of acceding to his demands. What the Spanish captain could not know was that an Acoma leader named Zutucapan saw nothing but woe for his people under Spanish rule and had convinced them to resist.

On the morning of December 4, the Acomans attacked. Zutucapan personally crushed Zaldívar's skull with his club; another 12 Spaniards were slain or fell to their deaths from the cliffs of the mesa. The Spaniards prepared their vengeance with all due attention to legalities. Formal proceedings were brought before the alcalde, or mayor, of San Gabriel. The "rebels" were tried *in absentia,* their treacheries enumerated, and their guilt pronounced. The friars declared the coming punitive expedition to be a "just war." Juan de Zaldívar's brother, Vincente, was chosen to mount the assault. He wasted no time and was standing before Acoma with 70 selected men on the cold, clear afternoon of January 21.

What ensued was a murderous feat of arms. Vincente de Zaldívar and

Burnished by a glowing sunset, Acoma Pueblo sits 357 feet above the surrounding New Mexico desert. Its mesa-top perch gave Acoma protection from invaders until Juan de Oñate's men forced their way up the rocky walls in 1599, using a precarious stairway carved by the Indians (right).

his handful of men faced several thousand Indians, many of them warriors. The main path to the pueblo, nothing more than steps cut into the rock, twisted precariously up the cliff face. Zaldívar called on the Acomans to surrender. The Indians replied with rocks and arrows. The Spaniards posted guards around the mesa and retired for the night. The next day, they attacked.

Under the cover of harquebus fire, the bulk of the force started the wicked climb up the main path. Meanwhile, Zaldívar sent a dozen agile fighters to scale the naked rockface at another place. Clinging to hand- and toeholds, the men inched their way to the top and struck the Indians from the rear. About the same time, the primary force arrived at the mesa, and the slaughter began. At last, Zutucapan was slain, and the Spaniards swept over the mesa, killing without mercy. Hundreds of Indians surrendered. Zaldívar sent them down the mesa to be held as prisoners. But hundreds more remained in the kivas and other parts of the pueblo. The Spaniards hauled them out one by one and hacked them to pieces. The few holdouts burned to death when the Spaniards torched the pueblo. In all, some 800 Acomans had been slain.

Oñate sentenced every male survivor over the age of 25 to have one foot severed as well as to serve 20 years of slavery. Males between the ages of 12 and 25 were condemned to 20 years of slavery, while younger children were distributed among the friars and Vincente de Zaldívar for "the salvation of their souls." Oñate ordered the women to be given to the Apache.

Still consumed with finding treasure, Oñate proceeded to loot all the pueblos within reach. He ordered that each town meet a quota of hides, blankets, and crops and confiscated even their sacred seed corn. As drought seared the land in the years 1600 and 1601, the pueblos descended into starvation.

The Spanish colonists were little better off. New

Struggling under their burdens, Indians are forced to carry the equipment of Spanish soldiers in this engraving dating from 1594. Finding no wealth to extract from the pueblos, a succession of Spanish governors of the 1600s exploited the Indians not only for manual labor but also by demanding tributes of food, clothing, and blankets.

Mexico had proved to be an unprofitable land. As the pueblos declined, the colonists went hungry, and talk of mutiny spread. Captain Luis de Velasco, who had contributed his personal fortune to the enterprise, smuggled a letter to the viceroy complaining of Oñate's tyranny. "The Indians fear us so much," wrote the captain, "that on seeing us approach from afar, they flee to the mountains with their women and children." Velasco described Oñate's cruel system of tribute. "The Spaniards seize their blankets by force, sometimes even when it is snowing, leaving the poor Indian women stark naked, holding their babes to their breasts." The colonists likewise stood in terror of the governor, he wrote. "We are all depressed, cowed, and frightened, expecting death at any moment."

Although the effect of this letter is not known, the frustrations of the colonists soon reached the boiling point. In June 1601, Oñate and his nephew departed San Gabriel with 70 men to continue the search for riches. The man he left in charge, Francisco de Sosa Peñalosa, found himself faced with rebellion. In a meeting, recorded by notaries, men kept silent too long came forth to vent their anger and testify to the lamentable state of affairs. One friar exclaimed that instead of preaching the word of God, "the Spaniards blaspheme it." His missionary work, he said, had encountered "great obstacles because of the bad treatment the Indians received from us. In order to induce the Indians to furnish corn, it has been necessary to torture the chieftains, even to hanging and killing them." The Indians, he said, were "starving to death, eating whatever filth there is in the fields, even the twigs from the trees, dirt, coal, and ashes." A second Franciscan commented that the treatment reflected "great discredit on our teachings, for they said that if we who are Christians caused so much harm and violence, why should they become Christian."

The meeting could have only one result. Early in October, the disillusioned colonists headed back down the Rio Grande trail. Despite the shabby treatment accorded them, the Indians supplied the Spaniards with grain and wild game; perhaps they simply wished to speed the strangers on their way. Only about 25 Spaniards remained at San Gabriel when Oñate returned on November 24. In a fury, he sent Vincente de Zaldívar racing south to arrest the traitors. But they were beyond reach.

Oñate was finished, although it took another six years of slow-moving Spanish justice to bring about his removal. Having achieved nothing in New Mexico, the king and his counselors were inclined to write off the costly experiment. But in the first decade of the new century, events were taking place that would encourage the Spaniards to stay.

The Pueblo peoples had recently suffered from raids by the Apache and other nomads, and the Indians' initial acceptance of Oñate may have stemmed in part from a desire for protection against these enemies. As it turned out, the Spaniards disrupted the traditional Indian trading network by stripping the pueblos of their surpluses. The goods and foodstuffs the Apache had been accustomed to receiving in trade were no longer available, and raiding became the prime method of obtaining necessities. Furthermore, the Spaniards had brought with them goods that widened Apache eyes—metal for tools and weapons, horses that could increase the mobility of a raiding party beyond all imagining. Some of these coveted items could be found in the pueblos where the Spaniards had bartered them for food. Within three years of Oñate's invasion, the pueblos suffered greater pressure than ever from the Apache. The only deterrent was the presence of Spaniards. As a result, more and more pueblo dwellers turned to the Christian God and the protection of the friars. In 1607 the friars working among the Rio Grande pueblos had counted only 400 baptisms. One year later, some 7,000 children and adults had taken the

Christian vows. They could not be abandoned. New Mexico would remain a colony, but at a reduced level with an initial complement of 50 married soldiers and a dozen Franciscan friars to protect and minister to the Indians.

The endeavor started well enough. Shortly after arriving late in 1609, Don Pedro de Peralta, Oñate's successor, moved the headquarters from San Gabriel to a salubrious site located about 30 miles to the southeast. There, he constructed Santa Fe as a proper Spanish town, obviating the need to dispossess Indians. Moreover, the Spaniards laid out fields to produce food, reducing another source of friction. In return for their services, the soldier-settlers received land grants, or encomiendas, as well as the right to exact labor and tribute from the Indians living on the property in return for Spanish protection.

The primary function of the colony was to support the missionaries. A Franciscan friar, in addition to his vestments and altar accouterments, carried tools with which to build his church, farm and household implements, and surgical equipment and medical supplies for his flock. The Franciscans taught their converts European construction techniques and other practical skills such as weaving, carpentry, leatherwork, and metalwork. They also showed the Indians how to raise livestock. Before long, the friars were shipping products for sale in Mexico. The enterprise flourished for two decades. By 1620 the 16 friars in New Mexico counted 17,000 converts; six years later, the books showed 20,181 Christian Indians worshiping at no fewer than 27 churches, 13 of them equipped with pipe organs.

Nevertheless, the price of this missionary success weighed heavily on the pueblos. Securing the necessities of life had always been difficult. Now the Indians faced the exhausting labor required to support twin sacred and secular Spanish establishments. Worse, the demands of Christian discipline soon came into sharp conflict with Indian beliefs and sacred obligations. The church doctrine of salvation, for example, was entirely foreign to the Indians. For the Pueblo peoples, the hereafter lay below, not in a heaven on high, and all expected to return to life in the underworld regardless of what they had done on earth. And whereas the friars drew on biblical tradition for their ethical guidelines, the Indians

Despite the influence of Christianity under Spanish rule, most Indians of the Southwest continued to maintain their ancient spiritual traditions. This Hopi doll, carved from the root of a cottonwood tree, was made to teach children the significance of one of the supernatural beings, or kachinas, that figure in Hopi religious ceremonies.

based their behavior on the pragmatic needs of the community, as established by their pantheon of gods. The Indians were content to add Christian ritual to their own complex ceremonials, but the Franciscans rejected all compromise involving Christian doctrine and punished recalcitrant Indians with floggings, imprisonment, enslavement, even execution.

The Franciscans showed themselves no less rigorous in their dealings with the colonists. Under the terms of the royal benefaction, the mission was entirely independent of secular control, and from the start, the holy men reacted with belligerence to the governors. In 1613 Father Isidoro Ordóñez, chief among the Franciscans, objected so violently to the collection of tribute from the Indians by civil authorities that he excommunicated Governor Peralta, then arrested him and threw him in chains when he tried to leave for Mexico City. Ordóñez continued the quarrel with Peralta's successors to the point where the Crown in 1620 rebuked both sides and issued new orders to end the disputes. The Franciscans were reminded that they had no right to interfere with the collection of tribute from the pueblos. The governors, for their part, were to enforce the rules stipulating that Indians be paid fair wages, that they be recompensed promptly for livestock damages to their property, and that their women not be abused. The Spanish viceroy's palace was hundreds of miles from Santa Fe, however, and neither the Franciscans nor the governors paid the admonitions much heed.

If the Franciscans were driven by an excess of zeal, the governors of the colony distinguished themselves mainly by a venality that was shocking to the Indians, who vested leadership in their bravest and wisest men. Between 1609 and 1680, the royal appointees methodically looted the province, stealing the livestock and goods of both Indians and settlers. But the real wealth was to be found in slaves. The busy silver mines of Mexico devoured laborers, and the Spanish governors set out to fill the demand by leading expeditions against the Plains tribes, who responded by raiding the pueblos under Spanish control.

Virtually every wagon train rolling south with goods from the pueblo workshops was accompanied by columns of captive Indians, lashed together with ropes. The men would be auctioned off to mine owners, the mothers and children sold as servants, the prettiest young women destined for brothels. The count of enslaved Indians swelled steadily. Part of the growth was attributable to the Apache, who preyed on other tribes, selling their captives at the large trading center of Pecos.

In the meantime, lack of rain and such diseases of the white man as smallpox added to the plight of the pueblo dwellers. Many villages ceased to exist altogether. Of the 100 or so pueblos that dotted the area at the coming of Coronado in 1540, only about 50 were still occupied a century later.

In 1666 a new cycle of drought seared the land. Over the next few years, many pueblo dwellers were reduced to eating animal hides that had been boiled with roots and herbs. A mysterious disease killed livestock as well as people; Apache and Navajo raiders stripped away the remaining animals, and by 1672, New Mexico was virtually devoid of cattle, sheep, and pigs.

As ordeal piled atop ordeal, the Native Americans turned to resistance. Indian anger had boiled to the surface in earlier times of stress; during a series of droughts in the 1630s and 1640s, a number of pueblos had murdered their missionaries and destroyed church property. Now, a handful of southern pueblos flared into open rebellion, killing Spaniards and raising havoc. These insurrections were quashed, but the spark had been struck for a general uprising.

The Indian leaders, typically, were the pueblo priests who still conducted their kiva ceremonies in direct defiance of the Franciscans. The friars had been powerless to purge the ancient beliefs, and in 1675, when a half-dozen friars and settlers died under mysterious circumstances, the Spaniards blamed the medicine men. The governor dispatched soldiers to

Scenes depicting the path to conversion for 18th-century Indians reflect the trials endured by the Pueblos 100 years earlier. They first present themselves for baptism (top left); next, they suffer punishments for such sins as witchcraft and lechery (lower left). Later, they gather to hear the word of God (top right), and are then led by a Spanish official to be baptized (lower right).

arrest the leaders, confiscate their religious paraphernalia, and burn their kivas. A good many escaped, but 47 were captured and carted to Santa Fe, where they were charged with witchcraft and sorcery, heinous crimes under Spanish law. All of them were brutally whipped, and as the trials progressed, three were hanged for refusing to pledge obedience; another committed suicide rather than submit.

But the pueblo dwellers were not intimidated. One day, a swarm of Indians appeared at Santa Fe, and 70 leaders entered the governor's palace to request an audience. Weapons in hand, they announced that they would not relinquish their traditions and demanded the release of their holy men; otherwise, they said, they would abandon the pueblos and join the Apache and Navajo in exterminating the Spaniards. The governor, Juan Francisco de Treviño, easily understood the arithmetic. Some 2,800 Spaniards of all ages were scattered about New Mexico; the Pueblo Indians numbered around 17,000, and no one could guess how many Apache and Navajo warriors lived beyond. Treviño released the medicine men. They returned to the pueblos to plot the demise of the Spaniards more vigorously than before. Among them was a middle-aged medicine man of incandescent hatred and outstanding organizational ability. His name was Popé. The Spaniards would wish that they had hanged him.

Although he was a native of San Juan Pueblo, Popé's immediate constituency was the pueblo of Taos, about 50 miles north of Santa Fe. From

Excavated from two New Mexico pueblos, a 17th-century glazed mug and bowl show the Spanish influence on traditional Indian pottery making.

there, over the next four years, he forged an alliance with other pueblo leaders and began planning a rebellion. Delegates found him in the darkness of the kiva, communing with three dancing figures, whose bodies glowed white and whom Popé identified as underworld spirits. So secret was the plotting that no woman was told anything about it, and when Popé suspected his own son-in-law of being too friendly with the Spaniards, he ordered his death as a lesson to would-be informers. At last, the date for the revolt was set for August 11, 1680. Couriers were dispatched to the pueblos, each with a length of cord with knots announcing the number of days remaining until the attack.

For all Popé's persuasion, a number of pueblos declined to participate. Some leaders cherished peace above all; others valued Christianity or had developed ties to the Spanish community. Thus it was that on August 9, the Spaniards learned of the imminent revolt from several pueblos. When word got back to Popé, he ordered an attack for sunrise next morning, August 10, and sent runners to inform the pueblos.

The missionaries were the first to die. Painted for battle, the warriors of Tesuque, nine miles north of Santa Fe, killed their padre outside the village when he came looking for them to say Mass. A friar in Jemez Pueblo succumbed as he knelt embracing a crucifix; another Franciscan was bound naked on the back of a hog and paraded through the pueblo to his place of execution. Three more priests perished at Zuni. In San Juan, San Ildefonso, Nambe, and a dozen other sites, priests were murdered, their churches defiled and burned.

Bands of Indians overran scores of isolated haciendas, torturing and killing Spaniards without regard to age or sex. Virtually every pueblo in the northern district had risen. At Taos, only two of the 70 or more Spaniards escaped; in the Picuris district, no one survived. When reports of the slaughter began filtering in, Governor Antonio de Otermín sent out small parties of soldiers to bring back survivors. Many settlers closer to Santa Fe managed to evade the attackers and find sanctuary in the capital, which Otermín was busily fortifying.

Meanwhile, to the south, Don Alonso García, the colony's lieutenant governor, led a contingent of soldiers to rescue settlers in those districts. He counted 120 corpses littering the road in the vicinity of Santo Domingo, and along another eight-mile stretch near Sandia, all of the Spaniards in 17 haciendas had been slain. At length he reached Isleta, one of the few pueblos that had refused to join the revolt. Seeking refuge there were

1,500 people. No fewer than 400 Spanish men, women, and children and 21 padres had met death at the hands of the Pueblo Indians.

On August 15, more than 500 Indians appeared before Santa Fe itself, some of them wearing Spanish armor stripped from the dead and carrying Spanish spears, swords, and guns. Governor Otermín asked for a parley, and a familiar Indian came forward. The Spaniards knew him as Juan, and heretofore had believed him loyal. He carried two crosses, one painted red signifying war, the other painted white for surrender. "We have killed your God and Santa María, and the king must yield, too," announced Juan in fluent Spanish. If the Spaniards chose red, they would be slaughtered; if they accepted white, they would be allowed to depart.

Otermín scorned both crosses and ordered an attack. By nightfall, his soldiers had repulsed the Indians, who burned and looted Santa Fe's outlying buildings as they retreated. By dawn, the Spaniards could see that the besiegers had been reinforced and now numbered nearly 2,000 warriors. On the 16th, the Indians swarmed into Santa Fe. The Spaniards controlled only the heart of the city: the plaza, the governor's palace, and a few buildings around it. Shrewdly, the Indians cut off the acequia supplying the city center with water; several times, Otermín's soldiers rushed out to retake the water source, but could not break through.

On August 18, Otermín launched a last desperate sally. Bursting out of the palace, he and 100-odd soldiers hurled themselves on the Indians, blasting with their harquebuses, slashing, spearing, and trampling the enemy beneath the hoofs of their horses. The suddenness and ferocity of the charge took the Indians by surprise; 300 died and another 47 were captured before the rest fled. Only five Spaniards were lost, although many suffered wounds, including Otermín.

The victory accomplished little. The burned-out capital was still surrounded, its defenders hopelessly outnumbered. The only salvation lay in retreating down the Rio Grande 300 miles to Mexico. On August 21, Otermín ordered the 47 prisoners executed. Then, he led a ragged procession of 1,000 settlers and soldiers out of Santa Fe.

At any point, a concerted onslaught could have overwhelmed the convoy. Groups of warriors dotted the hills lining the Rio Grande Valley. But they did not attack. Possibly the bloody reversal suffered in Santa Fe had given them pause; more likely, the Indians considered the exodus an acceptance of the white cross. In any event, Otermín and his people reached Isleta around September 3 after two harrowing weeks. On September 29, the last of the refugees reached safety near El Paso del Norte.

It was the first—and would prove to be the last—time that North American Indians succeeded in driving the Europeans out of a major domain. But the joy among the pueblo dwellers was short lived. For it soon became apparent that they had exchanged one tyrant for another. Pueblo tradition does not record what role, if any, Popé played in the actual fighting. But with the departure of the Spaniards, the medicine man moved swiftly to establish precisely the sort of centralized rule that had so aggrieved the independent-minded pueblos. He may have thought that after his success in unifying the pueblos against the Spaniards he could weld his people into one powerful nation. The results were calamitous.

Establishing himself in Governor Otermín's Santa Fe palace, Popé declared: "The God of the Christians is dead. He was made of rotten wood." Whereupon he set out to obliterate everything Spanish. Every church was now demolished, every cross, image, and reliquary fed into the flames. Christianized Indians scrubbed themselves clean of the taint of baptism with the suds of the yucca plant; those wearing rosaries and crosses were commanded to remove and smash them. Christian names were abolished, Christian marriages dissolved. No one was to utter another word of Spanish. The white man's plants were discarded as well. Peaches, onions, watermelons, grapes, peppers, apples, plums, lemons, and oranges, even wheat—all were uprooted and cast away. Henceforth, the pueblo diet would be as before: maize, squash, and beans. The Indians slaughtered the remaining livestock and left the carcasses to rot. They released the horses from the corrals—to be quickly collected by Plains tribes.

Popé costumed himself in gaudy robes and affected a bull's horn on his forehead to symbolize power. On occasion, he had himself drawn through the streets in Otermín's old carriage and staged parodies of Spanish feasts. He enslaved Indians who had not taken up arms or who dared to disobey his orders. He jailed or executed political foes and levied crushing tribute against any pueblo thought to oppose his rule.

RIO CHAMA VALLEY, NEAR RIO GRANDE

VESTIGES OF
CONQUEST

When the Spaniards entered the Southwest, the desert terrain was already dotted with the ruins of villages depleted by drought or strife. From the abandoned settlements had come refugees who swelled the pueblos, many of them favorably situated along the fertile banks of the Rio Grande or its tributaries, such as the Rio Chama *(above)*. Drawn to those havens, the Spaniards confidently proclaimed a new Christian millennium by erecting churches and crucifixes close to the kivas. Yet hunger, discord, and disease condemned a number of the mission pueblos to a short life and endowed New Mexico with relics of a different order, pictured here—testaments to the uneasy convergence of two proud cultures.

MISSION OF SAN JOSÉ AT JEMEZ PUEBLO

NUESTRA SEÑORA DE LA PURÍSIMA CONCEPCIÓN AT QUARAI PUEBLO

SAN BUENAVENTURA AT GRAN QUIVIRA PUEBLO

KUAUA PUEBLO RUINS

SAN GREGORIO AT ABO PUEBLO

All of this the pueblos might have suffered had the gods been kind regarding the weather. But Popé's kachina masks and ceremonial dances were no more effective than Franciscan prayers in bringing rain, and the drought continued. The pueblo world shrank to a few dozen weary towns along the river from Taos to just above present-day Albuquerque, plus Acoma, and the Hopi and Zuni villages to the west.

The year 1688 marked the death of Popé. By some accounts, he was murdered by his own disaffected people. His successor was a chieftain named Tupatú. Formerly a Christian who had been given the baptismal name of Luis, Tupatú had been one of Popé's principal lieutenants during the insurrection but had subsequently distanced himself from his erstwhile leader. In the years to come, Tupatú was destined to play an important role in the fortunes of his people. For the Spaniards were again headed north into New Mexico.

The last conquistador was a superb soldier and devoted servant of

Indians celebrate San Geronimo Day at Taos Pueblo, where the medicine man Popé first gathered support for the Pueblo Revolt of 1680. The warriors who rose up against the Spaniards carried rawhide shields such as the one below, discovered in the palace of the governor in Santa Fe after the revolt.

Spain with the grand name of Don Diego José de Vargas Zapata Luján Ponce de León y Contreras. The Spaniards had not forgotten about their lost province after the humiliation of 1680. The very next year, Governor Otermín made a valiant but unsuccessful attempt to retake the land. Two other expeditions had gone north in 1687 and 1688, but were forced to retreat. As soon as be became governor in 1690, Vargas lost not a moment in devising a plan to recolonize the province. He left El Paso in August of 1692. With him were fewer than 200 men—60 or so soldiers and about 100 pueblo warriors who had remained loyal to Spain, plus servants, grooms, and three friars eager to resume their missionary work. They rode through an empty landscape and pressed on to Santa Fe, reaching it on September 13.

The Indians still living in the old capital had erected pueblo dwellings and kivas among the roofless hulks of the Spanish buildings. The Spaniards went about their preparations, cutting the acequia supplying the city, emplacing a pair of bronze cannon, and laying charges of gunpowder against the city walls. But Vargas gave no order to attack. Instead, he parleyed with the Indians. He had come in peace, he called out. He urged them to surrender and promised that they would not be punished and could retain their leaders. He showed them a cross and a rosary, and pointed to the three friars who would give absolution.

At first the Indians were disbelieving and scornful. But as the day wore on, other Indians arrived from the north and, upon listening to Vargas, decided to make peace. Some of them entered Santa Fe, and after some time, a number of Santa Fe's defenders emerged from the city. Vargas greeted them with friendliness. Soon, other Indians came out, and all hostility evaporated. The friars ventured into Santa Fe to bestow blessings. Vargas himself was surrounded by a swarm of Indians, begging forgiveness. Vargas offered peace, as he later wrote, "with great love, as I stood there dismounted, embracing them, shaking hands with them, and speaking to them with tender and loving words."

On September 16, Tupatú arrived with 300 mounted warriors. He was impressively garbed in an old Spanish uniform adorned with animal skins, turquoise ornaments, and seashells; on his head was a sort of crown made from mother-of-pearl. Vargas, dressed in court costume, invited the chieftain—Don Luis now—to confer over biscuits and hot chocolate. The two exchanged gifts, and Vargas promised not to interfere with Tupatú's leadership so long as he helped return the pueblos to allegiance. Tupatú was back the next day with the leaders of the pueblos that accepted his authority. All knelt to receive amnesty and swear fealty.

By the time Vargas set out again for El Paso in December to gather up his colonists, he could claim to have repacified 73 pueblos. And the friars had performed 2,214 baptisms and rededicated numerous churches.

Many Indians saw Vargas as a savior who had ended the years of chaos. But there were others who detested the Spaniards, and one of these, a mestizo named Tapia, spent the winter denouncing them. The Spanish promises were nothing but lies, insisted Tapia. He predicted that when Vargas returned, he would slaughter the pueblo leaders. More than a few Indians believed him; the massacres perpetrated by Oñate and other Spaniards were still fresh. When Vargas returned with the first of his settlers late in 1693, he faced renewed hostility.

His expedition of 800 soldiers, settlers, and padres reached Santa Fe on December 16, amid bitter weather and reports of disaffected pueblos everywhere. At a meeting en route, Luis Tupatú had explained how angry his people were over Tapia's accusations. Vargas was confident that he could reason with the chiefs. In the meantime, there was the problem of his cold and hungry people.

The reception by the Indians in Santa Fe had been cool, and it grew chillier when Vargas informed them that they were illegally occupying a city built by Spaniards for Spaniards. When the Indians declined to leave, Vargas gave them one week, during which the colonists camped outside in the cold. At last, his own patience at an end, Vargas gave the Indians one last chance to decamp. When this brought jeers, he launched an assault on December 29 backed by Indian auxiliaries.

By nightfall the Spaniards had blasted through the city's defenses with only light casualties, while the defenders had suffered grievously. Sometime that night, their wounded chief hanged himself, and when the Spaniards renewed the attack before dawn, the Indians surrendered.

There was no mercy in Vargas's heart on this day. He ordered 70 of the leaders shot and another 400 Indians bound into 10 years of servitude. His hope of peaceful reconciliation was ended. Those Indians who

After the Spaniards fled their lands in 1680, Pueblo Indians made special use of what the invaders left behind. In Indian hands, pieces of European pottery became a spindle whorl (top), a bone scraper (bottom left), and a tear-shaped pendant (bottom right).

saw a virtue in the Spaniards could not argue against Tapia, whose warnings took on the stature of prophecy. Pecos and a few other pueblos remained loyal; Tupatú, who had renewed his pledge of allegiance, stood firm with what power he still possessed. The others fortified themselves atop their mesas. Vargas would have to reconquer them one by one, as his colonists struggled to establish themselves in this hostile land.

It took Vargas and his Indian allies most of the year to recapture the pueblos. The last stronghold to fall was the Black Mesa of San Ildefonso, a looming natural fortress held by warriors from a half-dozen pueblos. Vargas had failed to take the mesa during a two-week siege in March. Emboldened, the warriors began descending in darkness to raid the livestock corrals at Santa Fe. On September 4, Vargas tried again; this time his strategy included destroying the Indians' crops in the fields below the mesa. Faced with starvation, the warriors surrendered on September 8.

"With full sails we forge ahead," Vargas wrote his viceroy. But while the colonists farmed the land and the Indians again took up the white man's religion, language, and technology, peace remained fragile. When a poor harvest in 1695 depleted grain reserves, Indians and Spaniards alike died for lack of nourishment. By the spring of 1696, sparks of rebellion once more crackled through the dry New Mexican air.

As before, the missionaries felt the first blows. On June 4, 1696, the pueblos of Taos, Jemez, San Ildefonso, Nambe, and San Cristóbal each put their lone friars to death and burned their churches: 21 soldiers and settlers died too. Yet this was not to be a repetition of 1680. In fear of reprisal, the Indians of the affected pueblos immediately abandoned their homes after killing the friars and either took refuge with the Zuni and Hopi to the west, or fortified themselves in the hills along the Rio Grande. There were no attacks on Santa Fe or the outlying Spanish settlements. In a number of loyal pueblos, the leaders dealt swiftly with mutinous factions. At the time of the outbreak, three rebel leaders from Jemez and Nambe were recruiting in

The inscription on a formal portrait of Don Diego José de Vargas, the conquistador who persuaded defiant Pueblo Indians to surrender amicably to Spanish rule in 1692, celebrates Vargas's role as a peacekeeper. Yet when the Indians rebelled again a year afterward, Vargas crushed their revolt and had scores of their leaders shot.

Pecos; the loyal native governor of Pecos named Filipe hanged one of them and hauled the other two off to jail in Santa Fe. During the summer, he hanged another four rebels in his pueblo and beheaded a fifth.

By the end of 1696, the uprising had been crushed. Vargas treated the vanquished Indians with kindness, pardoned their leaders, and prepared to get on with the business of building New Mexico. But Vargas himself was fated to suffer a setback. His five-year term as governor was to expire that year, and he had requested a second term. Yet King Charles II inexplicably appointed in Vargas's stead a certain Don Pedro Rodríguez Cubero—who was more than happy to see his predecessor discredited.

Upon Rodríguez Cubero's arrival, a number of secret enemies denounced their former leader—for his refusal to give settlers Indian lands, for his prohibitions against forced Indian labor, for his insistence on pardoning rebellious Indians. They falsely accused him of embezzling funds and selling supplies for profit. Vargas was arrested, found guilty, and imprisoned in the Santa Fe palace. He spent three years behind bars, the last four months in chains, before a friendly Franciscan told the viceroy in Mexico City of the injustice. Vargas was ordered released, and late in 1703, he was restored to the governorship, with the title of marquis as recompense. He set about repairing the damages to the colony wrought by Rodríguez Cubero. But he was 61 years old, and in April 1704, he took ill and died, while on campaign with pueblo allies against the Apache.

The campaign against the nomadic raiders established a pattern. Henceforth, instead of fighting the Spaniards, the pueblos joined them against the common enemy. There were few options. Drought, disease, and internal strife had weakened the pueblos to the point where no energy remained for armed resistance to the white men. Populations continued to erode for the rest of the century. The Zuni pueblos, with a population of several thousand people in 1630, were reduced to 1,500 within 50 years, and by the mid-18th century, to fewer than 200 people. Most of the other pueblos withered by one-half or more. The Spanish community in New Mexico, on the other hand, grew to 20,000 settlers by 1800.

In accommodating the Spaniards, the surviving pueblos earned a measure of prosperity. By royal decree, they were made secure in their lands and labor; never again was the hated encomienda imposed to rob them of their efforts. With improved irrigation techniques acquired from the Spaniards, pueblo farmers raised a cornucopia of crops that once again were accepted as legitimate food. A wealth of chickens, goats, sheep, and cattle became theirs, and horses, mules, and two-wheeled carts revolutionized transport. Moreover, in learning Spanish, the many-tongued pueblos acquired a lingua franca.

Yet the Indians clung to their traditions. The pueblo councils continued to make major decisions, while the people tolerated the village officials installed by the Spaniards. Although the Indians dutifully attended Mass, and the friars baptized, married, and buried them, the kiva remained an ineluctable part of life. The Indians were careful to be discreet, and the Franciscans at last seemed to abide the coexistence of Indian and Christian customs. The Indians were allowed to worship in peace—and that, at least, was a victory for the spirits to smile upon. ✥

In this detail from an early-18th-century hide painting, a mounted Indian militia established by Spanish authorities attacks an Apache village. Alliances between the Spaniards and the Pueblos against mutual enemies were to become increasingly common.

MISSION TO CALIFORNIA

In 1769 an expedition of Spanish priests, soldiers, and Christianized Indians ventured north from the settled Baja peninsula into the wilds of Alta California, armed with a mandate "to establish the Catholic faith, to extend Spanish domain," and "check the ambitious schemes of a foreign nation." Russian fur traders had recently begun filtering down the Pacific Coast from the Aleutian Islands, and the Spaniards feared their claim to Alta California might be challenged if they failed to establish a presence there. In this last imperial thrust by the Spaniards in North America, gray-robed Franciscan friars were the quiet conquistadors. Working in pairs and aided by small numbers of troops, they founded 21 missions within a half-century, baptized 54,000 Indians, and altered native life irrevocably.

Unlike earlier efforts in New Mexico, where friars found existing pueblos and built churches there, the Franciscans in California encountered a far-flung population of hunter-gatherers and proceeded to "reduce," or concentrate, them at mission compounds, where Indians were expected to adopt Spanish speech and customs along with the Christian faith. The transition was traumatic, but some ancestral ways endured. Heeding the hard lessons of the Pueblo Revolt, many friars tolerated Indian dances on holidays and turned a blind eye to other tribal practices. "Though all are Christians," one visitor remarked of the mission Indians in 1827, "they still keep many of their old beliefs, which the padres, from policy, pretend not to know."

Following Sunday Mass, Indians in traditional dress celebrate their own rites at San Francisco's Mission Dolores in 1816. One spectator observed that the performers "paint their bodies with regular lines of black, red, and white. The men dance six or eight together, all making the same movements, all armed with spears."

From San Diego to San Francisco, the missions of Alta California were melting pots for the region's numerous coastal tribes, whose cultures were so diverse that a single mission might include converts speaking as many as five different languages.

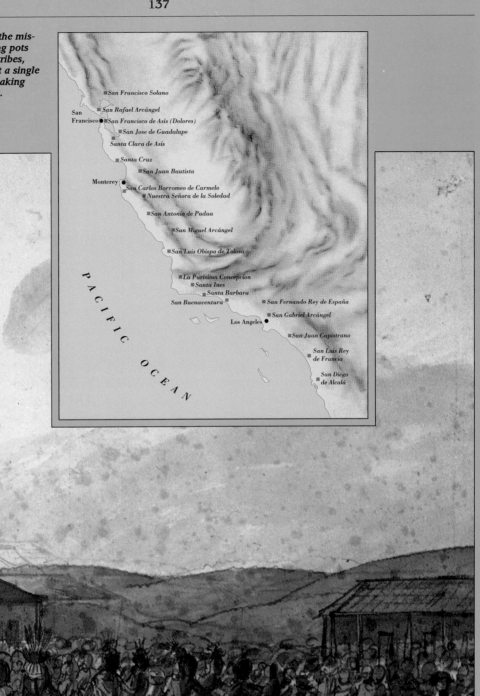

San Francisco Solano
San Rafael Arcángel
San Francisco — San Francisco de Asís (Dolores)
San Jose de Guadalupe
Santa Clara de Asis
Santa Cruz
San Juan Bautista
Monterey — San Carlos Borromeo de Carmelo
Nuestra Señora de la Soledad
San Antonio de Padua
San Miguel Arcángel
San Luis Obispo de Tolosa
La Purísima Concepcion
Santa Ines
Santa Barbara
San Buenaventura — San Fernando Rey de España
San Gabriel Arcángel
Los Angeles
San Juan Capistrano
San Luis Rey de Francia
San Diego de Alcalá

PACIFIC OCEAN

A mounted Spaniard charges a defiant trio of Costanoan Indians in this stylized sketch done in 1791. Although some local groups opposed the Spanish settlements, they were unable to form multitribal alliances and were easily crushed by the Spanish military.

ANGLING FOR SOULS

Once friars had selected a mission site, they began what one priest called "spiritual fishing"—luring Indians with glass beads and other bait. Although church doctrine opposed conversion by force, overzealous troops sometimes rounded up prospects. Friars told converts that they would have to remain at the mission unless granted leave, but more than a few Indians chafed at the routine and fled, only to be pursued by Spanish troops or armed converts. If some Indians were restrained by fear or bound by faith, many stayed on at the missions out of necessity as their native economy collapsed under the impact of European diseases and a deluge of Spanish goods that devalued local wares such as shell beads—a time-honored medium of exchange.

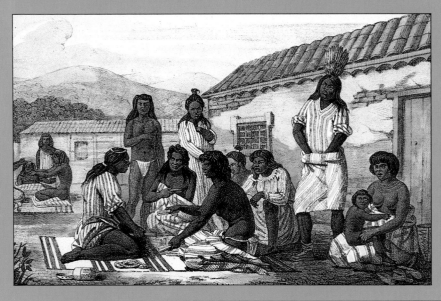

Indians gamble with sticks at Mission Dolores in 1816. A visitor noted that the participants— who were forbidden to wager their clothing—bet with small white shells that served as money.

Spanish lancers oversee Indian work crews outside the San Francisco presidio, one of four forts erected along the coast. In addition to toiling in mission fields and workshops, converts were farmed out to presidios. Reported one friar in 1825: "The Indians are complaining bitterly at having to work that the soldiers may eat."

An idyllic view of the Mission San Gabriel in 1832 portrays both an Indian reed hut and adobe barracks (background, left), designed to bring converts closer to the fold. The distinctive tile roofs of mission buildings were introduced after hostile Indians burned the thatch roofs of several early structures.

THE NATIVE LEGACY

Mission Indians placed their conspicuous stamp on their new culture. Trained as musicians and artisans by friars and Mexican craftsmen, the converts combined those acquired skills with ancestral talents and developed a distinctive artistic style of their own. Those Native Americans who decorated mission churches, for example, broadened their palettes by supplementing imported pigments with local ones that had been used traditionally for rock painting and body adornment. "The gaud of all this coloring," reported one traveler, "must have had a wondrous effect on the minds of the gazing Indians." Adding to the festive air of the Christian services was the presence of Indian bands, whose repertoire was as diverse as the color scheme of the surroundings. "It was not unusual," another churchgoer marveled, "to hear during the Mass the most lively dancing tunes."

143

Indian musicians—
dressed for a special
occasion—gather at
Mission San Buena-
ventura. Indians
mastering European
instruments drew
on their native expe-
rience with wooden
flutes, bone whistles,
and gourd rattles.

In a church painting significant for Indians under duress, Christ
bears his cross, harried by soldiers. The native artist, puzzled by the
idea of a mature Virgin, pictured Mary as a girl (hands clasped).

A host of colors adorns the church walls of
Mission San Miguel, painted by Indians under the guidance of artist Esteban Munras.
Some of the earthy hues that were used
for the decoration of churches came from
clays long gathered by Indians to paint
themselves for dancing or making war.

A RICH HERITAGE REDUCED

Beginning in 1833, the Mexican government, having recently won independence from Spain, took control of the missions and placed them in secular hands. Much of the property went to ranchers, and many of the churches fell into disrepair. Hard-pressed Indian converts, their ranks depleted by disease, now saw officials renege on promises to set them up as free landholders. With no tribal society to return to, most became peons for the ranchers. In the words of one friar, the outcome left mission Indians "demoralized and dispersed."

Debris litters the nave of the Carmel Mission after the collapse of its roof in 1851. Once home to 876 Indians, the mission land was sold in 1834, and the church was left to decay. A visitor a few decades later found it haunted by cattle, squirrels, and flocks of birds nesting in the deserted walls.

This Chumash Indian couple, shown in the early 1880s, was among those in Santa Barbara who continued to frequent the mission church (background) after the surrounding land was sold in 1846. The fate of the Chumash, whose domain extended up the coast from Ventura to San Luis Obispo, was typical of mission Indians. Numbering at least 10,000 when the friars arrived, they had been reduced to about 2,500 when the missions were secularized. A century afterward, fewer than 100 Chumash remained in all of California.

4

INTRUDERS ON PACIFIC SHORES

This carved wooden helmet, portraying a fiercely grinning figure with teeth of shell and whiskers of fur, was worn by a Tlingit warrior whose tribe clashed with Russian fur traders when they encroached on its domain in the early 1800s. Such helmets served both to intimidate opponents and to deflect blows from war clubs.

The hunt typically began at dawn early in the summer, when the sea was calmest. It was a spectacle that never failed to impress the Russians who flocked to the Aleutian Islands in the 18th century in search of furs. The hunters, a dozen or so stocky, fierce-looking men whose ancestors had migrated long ago to these rugged volcanic outcroppings from the Alaskan mainland, would emerge from dugout houses. Intricate tattoos adorned their high cheekbones, and ornaments of bone protruded from their noses and lower lips. Atop their stiff black hair they wore painted wooden visors decorated with walrus whiskers or other emblems of their prowess. Long parkas made of the feathery down of puffins or other shorebirds kept out the chill; each garment consisted of up to 40 pelts, with the down worn next to the skin. Waterproof cloaks fashioned of whale or sea lion intestines completed their garb.

Thus girded against cold and wet, the Aleuts hefted onto their shoulders their one-man kayaks, 15-foot-long boats laboriously crafted from seal or sea lion skins sewn together and stretched over a light framework of wood or whalebone. At the water's edge, each hunter slipped into the open hatch of his sleek craft, gathered the covering close around his torso, and tied it fast to make his kayak watertight. Then he took up his double-bladed wooden paddle, with which he could propel his craft through choppy waters as fast as a sailing ship under a fresh breeze.

The Aleuts had been learning to maneuver their kayaks since they were young boys. They could slip in and out of coastal inlets through thick fog and treacherous currents, disdainful of rocks and reefs. They could flip their vessels over and then right them, "sporting about more like amphibious animals than human beings," in the words of an Englishman who visited the islands after the Russians claimed them. Hunting by kayak required patience as well as quickness, and the men could endure stints of as many as 12 hours in the cramped hatch.

The Aleuts stalked various creatures along the coast, including seals, sea lions, and walruses. But the quarry of most interest to the Russians

An Aleut hunting visor, its painted bentwood frame decorated with beads and two miniature carved puffins, sports a plume fashioned of beaded sea lion whiskers.

and other white men was the sleek-pelted sea otter, whose agile movements led the nimble kayakers to regard the animal as a kindred spirit. Tracking that elusive creature was a solemn and intricate ritual for the Aleuts. Paddling silently so as not to alert their prey, they deployed in a long line, spread out side by side to cover a broad area. The moment one of the hunters glimpsed the otter's dark shape at the surface, he raced to the spot and lifted his paddle high as a signal. The others formed a wide circle around the boatman. If the cunning otter had picked up the slightest sound or scent of danger, it would dive and remain submerged for minutes on end. The hunters waited patiently, weapons ready, knowing that otters seldom traveled farther underwater than the radius of their circle. Consummate marksmen who rarely missed their targets from distances up to 100 feet, the men were armed with spears or darts tipped with stone or bone. To launch the darts, the hunters carried a small version of the atlatl used by their Asian forebears—a throwing stick that hooked onto the butt of the weapon and whipped it forward with power when the hunter snapped his wrist.

As soon as the otter surfaced, the nearest Aleut hurled his weapon and shouted. This first quick shot might not hit the mark, but it forced the animal to dive before getting a good breath. Then the marksman took up position over that new spot and signaled formation of another, smaller circle. The hunt continued in this manner, with the circle narrowing until the exhausted quarry was dispatched with one or more wounds. By tradition, the man who first struck the otter laid claim to its carcass, although he would offer to share it with others back in the village. The resourceful Aleuts, who let little of value in their

A sea otter rests onshore in a 1788 drawing by a naturalist who accompanied Russian fur traders to the Aleutian Islands. Since sea otters seldom obliged hunters by coming to land, the Aleuts donned their visors and pursued them in kayaks (below), hurling darts or spears. The pelts proved so valuable that traders called them "soft gold."

environment go to waste, hunted the sea otter for its flesh as well as its pelt. Europeans considered otter meat unsavory, however, and coveted only the remarkable fur. Unlike other marine mammals, the sea otter lacked a thick layer of blubber and relied for insulation on its coat—the densest pelage of any furbearing animal. In addition to providing warmth by virtue of the air trapped between its fine hairs, the fur shone with a jet-black gloss, tinged silver at the roots. The pelt was so stunning, remarked William Sturgis, a ship captain from Boston, that only "a beautiful woman and a lovely infant" could rival it. The Chinese, in particular, prized the skins, fashioning them into splendid robes and capes.

Driven by Chinese demand, merchant ships ranged up and down the Northwest Coast, seeking sea otter pelts wherever the animal thrived, from Alaska to California. The Russians initiated the trade, in the Aleutians, but they were followed soon after by Spaniards, Britons, and Anglo-Americans, who confined their efforts primarily to lower latitudes. Much as the glitter of gold or the sheen of beaver pelts had exposed Indians elsewhere to fateful intrusions, the luster of sea otter fur now brought

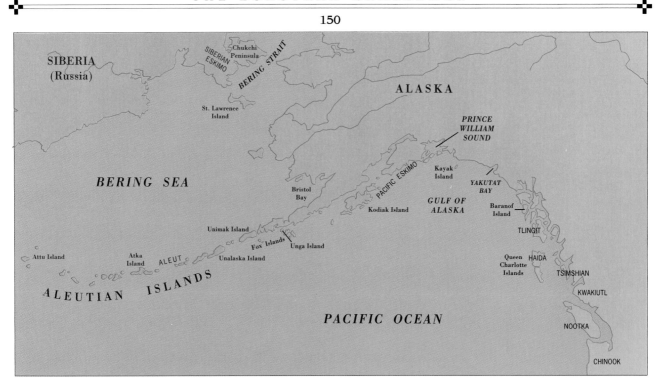

The maritime riches of the Northwest Coast, with its myriad islands and inlets, drew white explorers and fortune hunters into contact with a host of native cultures. Alaska's shores were frequented mainly by Russian traders, who finagled and often fought with the Aleuts on the Aleutians, the Koniags on Kodiak Island, and the Tlingit along the southeast coast. Farther south, proud tribal groups such as the Nootka of Vancouver Island bargained shrewdly with competing merchants from Spain, Great Britain, and the United States.

powerful forces to bear on the peoples of the Northwest. Here, however, local tribes beset by cunning traders often managed to hold their own through shrewd dealing and shows of force. Even when the outsiders used their superior weaponry to impose their will, as the Russians did in Alaska, the cultures they subjected were able to adapt and endure. In the end, large areas of the Northwest Coast would remain the province of tribal societies, modified but not submerged by European influences.

The Aleuts first encountered the Russians in 1741 when the explorer Vitus Bering, a Danish-born commander in the Russian navy, crossed the gulf known today as the Bering Sea, probed the southern coast of Alaska, and returned home on a path that brought him up against the Aleutian archipelago, jutting westward from the Alaska Peninsula. In September, near one of the islands in that long chain, two men in kayaks paddled out to his ship, gesturing toward land. The Russians dubbed these islanders Aleuts—a contraction of the name of a Siberian people they resembled.

The men on the ship offered one of the Aleut kayakers brandy and a lighted pipe of tobacco, but neither gift appealed to him. What apparently did make an impression on the islanders was a man from coastal Siberia whom the Russians had brought along as an interpreter. When the Siberian came ashore with a small party from the ship, Aleuts surrounded him, evidently fascinated by the similarity between his features and their own. The nervous Russians feared that the islanders might try to seize the man, and when some other Aleuts began to show a similar interest in their rowboat, members of the landing party fired their muskets over the heads of the astonished Indians and fled with their interpreter. As the Russians sailed away, one of Bering's men recalled, the Aleuts "waved their hands to us to be off quickly as they did not want us any longer."

Unfortunately for the Aleuts, these mystifying aliens with their fearsome weapons were not to be so easily dismissed. Bering would not return to Alaska, for he was near death from scurvy. But before he succumbed, his ship anchored off a body of land known later as Bering Island—beyond the western tip of the Aleutians—where his crew made a discovery that would entice Russians across the sea in droves. Although uninhabited, the island teemed offshore with sea otters, which the sailors duly harvested by shooting or clubbing them. The animal's flesh helped them survive the winter, and when they returned to Siberia the following year, a cache of 600 sea otter pelts repaid them for their sufferings.

News of this trove on the newly charted islands east of Siberia touched off a rush of fortune-hunting fur traders. The Russians were old hands at trapping fox, beaver, and other furbearing animals. Indeed, their conquest of Siberia during the previous century had been built on such quarry, especially the sable, whose dark brown pelt dominated the Chinese market before the boom in sea otters.

For all their experience on land, however, the Russian fur traders—known as *promyshlenniki*—were rank amateurs when it came to hunting for pelts at sea. At bases on Siberia's Kamchatka Peninsula, they cobbled together rickety ships of green timber held together with leather thongs, flexible whalebone, or willow switches, and rigged with sails of animal hide. Iron to bind the boats and sailcloth to propel them were impractical, because they had to be hauled from the distant Russian heartland.

More than a few traders who set out from Siberia in these makeshift vessels—capable of carrying as many as 60 men—were lost at sea. Those who survived soon discovered an attractive alternative to hunting sea otters off the treacherous reefs of Bering Island and other desolate spots. They pushed on to the Aleutian chain, where furbearing creatures were nearly as abundant and the traders could rely on native hunters with their agile kayaks and superb marksmanship.

Perhaps 20,000 people inhabited the scores of islands that made up the Aleutians, and the Russians treated them the same way they had the indigenous peoples of Siberia—with brute force. The techniques seldom varied. A ship landed, and several dozen armed promyshlenniki, often accompanied by native Siberians, stormed ashore. To make the Aleut men hunt for them, they whipped them or threatened them with muskets and seized their women and children as hostages. Only after the Aleuts

had met a quota of furs—which sometimes took months—did the Russians release the hostages. The traders typically paid for a portion of the furs with beads, goat's wool, hatchets, and other goods. They seized the rest as a tax, due the government in Saint Petersburg because the Aleuts were now considered subjects of imperial Russia. This further provoked the islanders, who had never been taxed by their own leaders but now had to pay tribute to an unseen foreign empress, Catherine the Great.

Most infuriating for the native peoples was the exploitation of their women. Although the promyshlenniki professed scorn for Aleut women, sneering at their tattoos, nose pins, and body lice, they frequently sought their company. Even before the holding of hostages became routine, the Russians acted as if the females they encountered were theirs for the taking. The first Russian party to reach Attu Island, the westernmost of the Aleutians, in 1745, demanded women as consorts, and when their men balked, gunned down 15 of them. "Wives are taken from their husbands,

A mother tends her child while her neighbors converse in one of the large, earth-and-straw-covered houses shared by several Aleut families on the island of Unalaska. This land was visited first by Russians and later by Englishmen, including artist John Webber, who drew this sketch in 1778 while on an expedition led by Captain James Cook. Within such houses, family groups had their own alcoves, fitted with a mat that could be let down to afford some privacy.

and daughters from their mothers," complained Martin Sauer, an Englishman on a geographical expedition for the Russian navy. Authorities in Saint Petersburg, who exercised little control over the traders, reprimanded one company of promyshlenniki for "indescribable outrages" and instructed them to desist from "barbarities, plunder, and ravaging of women."

Besides the lust of adventurers away from home, misperceptions about sexual customs led the Russians to take liberties. Aleuts occasionally prostituted women they had claimed as slaves during raids on other islands. And Aleut men purchased their wives and sometimes invited other males to enjoy their favors, but only as a way of satisfying an old obligation or imposing a new one. Mistaking these customs as evidence that the Aleuts had no scruples, the Russians and other European traders often violated tribal codes and drove the men to armed resistance.

Aleut villagers seldom quarreled among themselves, accustomed as they were to sharing the bounty of the hunt and settling disputes at communal gatherings presided over by a ruling elder the Russians termed the *toion,* or best man. Yet long-running feuds between rival settlements kept people primed for combat, and the same skills required for hunting made the menfolk formidable warriors when the need arose. As the Russians moved eastward along the Aleutian chain, they faced increasing resistance from groups who may have learned of Russian outrages from their neighbors to the west and were ready to strike back.

Early in 1762, Aleuts on Unga Island near the Alaskan mainland responded to Russian assaults on

Two meticulous Webber drawings depict inhabitants of Unalaska. The man, his nose and lower lip pierced with bone, wears a hunting visor decorated with whiskers, feathers, and a small effigy made of walrus tusk. The woman, her cheeks tattooed like other members of her sex, wears a sealskin frock and a string of beads suspended from her nose.

their women by carrying out attacks that killed eight traders and wounded several more. The surviving Russians fled, returning to Siberia with a cargo of 900 sea otter pelts and 25 young Aleut girls, who met with a cruel fate. When the ship reached the coast of Siberia, armed Russians escorted 14 of the girls ashore to pick berries. Two of them managed to escape, and an enraged officer then killed another girl on the spot, so upsetting the rest that they jumped from the boat carrying them back to the ship and drowned. Unnerved, the Russian officer tried to eliminate all traces of the incident by ordering the Aleut girls who had stayed on the ship thrown overboard—a crime that later surfaced during an inquest into the abuses of the trading company that sponsored the journey.

The uprising on Unga Island was just one in a series of native assaults on traders along the eastern reaches of the Aleutian chain. In June 1762, on Unalaska Island, Aleuts carried out simultaneous attacks on scattered Russians and Siberians, killing or wounding more than a dozen. The islanders synchronized their actions in ritual fashion by distributing an equal number of sticks to various war parties, who burned one stick in the fire each day. When the last stick went up in flames, they reached for their clubs and knives and lashed out at the nearest intruders.

The Russians escalated the violence. In 1764 a ruthless trader named Ivan Soloviev landed on Unalaska with a band of followers. Soloviev learned of the attacks there two years before as well as a wider rebellion by Aleuts on Unalaska and nearby islands in 1763, during which four Russian ships had been destroyed and more than 150 traders killed. Soloviev, whose own party repulsed an attack that cost the Aleuts 100 lives, set out to teach the locals a lesson by enlisting armed Russians in a campaign to lay waste the trouble spots. The men went from island to island, burning villages, destroying boats and stores of food, and overwhelming the Aleuts' hand-launched weapons with musketry and cannon fire.

The terrible climax came when Soloviev's forces attacked a fortified village on Unalaska Island where 300 Aleuts were gathered. When the defenders barricaded themselves, the Russians filled bladders of animal skin with gunpowder and planted them under the log walls. Aleut defenders who survived the explosions were cut down by bullets and saber thrusts. Soloviev's cruelty to captives became the stuff of grim legends. By one account, he lined up 12 Aleuts in a file, tied them together, and fired his musket at point-blank range to find out how many men a single shot would kill. The bullet reportedly stopped at the ninth man.

Soloviev's punishing offensive ended resistance on the Aleutians, but

ALASKA'S ENDURING ISLANDERS

During the time that they were living under Russian rule, roughly a century, the people of the Aleutian Islands adopted—or were forced to accept—a bewildering variety of foreign customs. They learned the Russian language, donned Russian clothes, gradually abandoned their semi-subterranean dwellings to live in box-like Russian-style houses, and even took Russian names—which most of the Aleutian islanders retain to this day.

Thousands of the indigenous peoples were converted to the Russian Orthodox faith by the priests who accompanied the traders. In addition, large groups of Aleuts were uprooted like so many serfs and sent off to hunt sea otters and seals in places such as the Pribilof Islands—rocky, wind-swept dots in the Bering Sea that presented an even more forbidding landscape than their native shores.

The Aleuts nevertheless managed to cling to many of their old ways, hunting and fishing in the ancestral fashion and observing time-honored family and communal ceremonies such as the festivals villagers staged to honor the spirits of the animals they hunted. The result of the accumulated influences was a unique cultural blend of native traditions and acquired traits that prevailed long after the Russians left the islands, as revealed in the photographs here and on the following pages, which were taken around 1900.

Shrouded with Russian babushkas, two Aleut women stand by the entrance to a dugout of the kind that was gradually replaced by the frame house.

Stalking prey much as their forebears did before the Russians arrived, two Aleut hunters in European dress paddle their kayak through placid waters off the Alaska Peninsula.

Aleuts in smocks and vests go about the grisly work of clubbing fur seals on the rocky shore of Saint Paul Island, largest of the Pribilofs. The Russians originally dispatched Aleuts to the Pribilofs on seasonal hunting expeditions, but some of the hunters eventually settled there with their families.

A bearded Russian priest (left)—still ministering to the Aleuts long after other Russian authorities have departed—stands beside newlyweds at the Orthodox church in the Pribilof village of Saint Paul, shown below with the church's onion dome spires dominating the neat houses. The Russians lured some Aleuts to the faith by excusing converts from paying taxes for three years.

elsewhere the torch of defiance burned on. In 1763 Russian traders had reached Kodiak Island, below the Alaska Peninsula, where they met with concerted opposition from the 3,500 or so Pacific Eskimo people known as Koniags, who lived there in large dugout homes made from the stout timber found on the island. With their tattoos, dangling lip ornaments, and other imposing flourishes, the Koniags appeared as menacing as the Aleuts to the Russians. In fact, they were even more formidable. Koniags were trained from childhood to endure hardship. Boys were made to stand for hours in cold seawater, to cut themselves with sharp shells, and even to pluck the innards from a captured and still-living enemy warrior. Men conditioned to such rigors were not about to yield when a few Russians rowed ashore and demanded hostages through an Aleut interpreter. The Koniags may not have understood all the interpreter was saying in his strange dialect, but they could see that the white men came as masters. And the islanders had no intention of providing them with slaves.

Shortly after this tense encounter, Koniag archers slipped down to the shore at daybreak and pelted the Russian ship with arrows before being dispersed by gunfire. Girding themselves for a second try, the warriors returned a few days later with large wooden shields, behind which they launched arcing shots from their bows. Again, Russian muskets kept the assailants at bay, and once more the Koniags refined their tactics. After elaborate preparations that consumed three weeks, they mounted a third attack behind massive wooden barricades, each of which sheltered 30 to 40 men. Braving a splintering hail of bullets, the attackers shoved their heavy screens down to the water's edge—close enough to the ship that the Russians feared it might be stormed and set afire. Desperate, the traders waded ashore and drove the Koniags back in close fighting.

Sapped by the struggle, the two sides observed an uneasy truce. The Russians held out through the winter, bartering now and then with Koniags for furs, but the take was meager compared to that gleaned elsewhere by exploiting native hunters. In the spring of 1764, the intruders departed, and few traders set foot on the island again for a generation.

When Russians finally returned to Kodiak in force two decades later, they arrived under new leadership with a fresh resolve. Alarmed by native resistance to unruly promyshlenniki, by the rapid depletion of sea otter colonies (whose females whelped just one pup a year), and by the prospect of competition in the northern Pacific from Spain and England, officials in Saint Petersburg were struggling to bring order to the fur trade. One bold group of Russian merchants thought they could do just that by

In a scene painted in 1804, a Russian fur ship coasts into a snug, settled harbor on Kodiak Island, once the site of fierce fighting between the traders and the native Koniags. By this time, Koniag hunters such as those paddling their kayaks in the foreground of the painting were in thrall to the Russian-American Company.

monopolizing the business. Leading their effort was Grigory Ivanovich Shelekhov, a veteran of the Aleutian trade who set out to replace the transient camps of the promyshlenniki with a string of permanent Russian outposts. For his first such colony, he chose Kodiak Island—a forbidding target, but one whose fur reserves remained largely untapped.

Shelekhov and 130 Russian colonists landed on Kodiak in 1784 and soon ran into resistance. Still convinced that the Russians meant to enslave them, the Koniags refused Shelekhov's assurances and gifts and adhered to what he called their "perverse and obstinate behavior," insisting that the Russians leave the island at once. When Shelekhov declined, the islanders attacked his camp, and the Russians had to bring up cannon to

This Koniag kayak paddle used during the era of Russian rule bears the images of an otter (lower right) and a mythical thunderbird attached to a circular rattle of the sort shaken by islanders during their ceremonial dances.

drive them off. Shelekhov's men then bombarded the village where the Koniag warriors sought refuge, taking a heavy toll. To discourage further resistance, Shelekhov staged a deceptive show of Russian might. As islanders looked on, one of his men fired a musket at a huge rock that had been drilled and packed with gunpowder. A terrific explosion pulverized the boulder, and Shelekhov reported proudly that the island was soon rife with rumors ''about the amazing strength of our marksmen.''

He then set about pacifying Kodiak Island. He kept 400 of the Koniag captives and put them to work hunting sea otters. In their double-holed kayaks, they demonstrated skills that rivaled those of the Aleuts. Although Shelekhov paid them for their labors, he made sure of their obedience by holding hostage many of their women and children. As a matter of policy, however, he discouraged the flagrant abuses that had poisoned Russian relations with the Aleuts. Instead, he tried to convert the Koniags to Russian ways. Knowing that Empress Catherine was concerned for the religious welfare of her new subjects, Shelekhov built a school for boys and imported Russian Orthodox priests to raise them in the faith. Such efforts, later duplicated on other islands in the region, endeared his firm to Saint Petersburg. Finally, in 1799, four years after

Shelekhov's death, the Russian-American Company he had helped foster was granted a monopoly by Emperor Paul I, giving it exclusive trading rights to the furs that Aleuts, Koniags, and other native peoples gathered so diligently.

Islanders who had at one time endured rape and plunder now faced systematic exploitation. The Russian-American Company secured its hold on native villages by enlisting their leaders as employees. Once the chiefs had signed on, agents rounded up Aleut and Koniag hunters; some 2,000 men were pressed into service every spring and summer. Families were disrupted as the hunters traveled ever farther south in pursuit of the dwindling sea otter, all the way to the coast of California. Defying Spain's claim to that area, the company in 1812 founded a short-lived settlement called Fort Ross north of San Francisco Bay, maintained by Aleuts who gathered furs and fish and raised vegetables.

Dislocation, disease, and warfare depleted the native societies of the arctic islands. By 1805, after four decades of contact with outsiders, the indigenous population on Kodiak had been halved. Among the Aleuts on Unalaska, the decrease amounted to two-thirds in just 25 years. Had the survivors been pressed by an onslaught of white settlers like beleaguered tribes elsewhere in North America, they might have been extinguished. But the rigors of life in the Far North attracted only small numbers of priests and officials, who imposed elements of their culture on the islanders without effacing their

Leader of the Tlingits who overran the Russian fort at Sitka in 1802, Chief Kotlean wears a woven spruce-root hat, a ceremonial blanket, and hide garments, as well as a Russian medal, likely given him as a peace token after Russians reclaimed the area in 1804 and built a new fort (background). With him is his wife, shown face front and in profile, with a protruding lip ornament.

heritage. Schools taught Russian as well as Aleut, and the distinctive spires of Russian Orthodox chapels sprouted on the harsh landscape. The samovar filled with tea from China became almost as familiar a sight in the dugout houses on Unalaska as in the parlors of Saint Petersburg.

Elsewhere along the Gulf of Alaska, a different pattern was emerging. By 1800 the assertive Russian-American Company was stretching its tentacles down Alaska's southeast coast, where barrier islands replete with coves and inlets promised fresh rewards. But the outfit's progress was impeded by the redoubtable Tlingit Indians, who dominated those islands and the adjacent mainland. Drawing on the area's lush woodlands, streams, and estuaries, the Tlingit had evolved a prosperous and well-organized culture that placed considerable power in the hands of village chiefs. Those leaders could deploy large bands of warriors who, like the Koniags, were taught from an early age to bear privation. And the Tlingit had material assets the Koniags and Aleuts lacked—firearms and powder, even small cannon, all obtained from English and American shipmasters who poached on turf claimed by the Russians and outbid them for sea otter furs. These traders willingly exchanged firearms because they had no desire to settle in the area.

The Russian-American Company first felt the fury of the well-armed Tlingit in 1802 when its outpost on the island the Indians called Sitka came under attack. The southernmost of several Russian forts located on or near the Alaskan mainland, the Sitka stronghold, called Saint Michael, had a year-round ice-free harbor and was meant to replace Kodiak as the company's administrative center in the New World. But the Tlingit had a fortified village of their own nearby and resented the intrusion. Plied with English guns, they waited until a large work detail of Russians had left the stockade, then stormed the buildings and set them afire, killing 20 Russians and 130 Aleut laborers and claiming 3,000 sea otter pelts.

Undaunted, the Russians returned with an armada in 1804 and pounded the Tlingit village until the Indians abandoned it. Company officials then built a second fort near the remains of the first and christened it New Archangel. The traders there faced constant harassment from the surrounding Tlingit and had to maintain a costly garrison of nearly 500 men and 150 cannon. Some Russians wed Tlingit women or consorted with them, unwittingly providing hostile Indians with informants in the company's camp. The Tlingit boasted that they only tolerated the presence of the Russians for the convenience of having a supply of trade goods. Neither commerce nor Russian Orthodox missionaries mellowed them. In 1839 a priest who had won many Aleut and Koniag converts was embarrassed to say that he could count only 20 baptized Tlingit at Sitka. When Alaska was sold to the United States three decades later, few Tlingit had been lured close enough to Mother Russia to mourn her departure.

Farther south along the Pacific Coast, Indians similar in character and culture to the Tlingit reacted opportunistically to the emerging fur trade. Such tribes as the Haida of the Queen Charlotte Islands, the Kwakiutl of coastal British Columia, and the Nootka of Vancouver Island all were disciplined, socially stratified groups whose village chiefs sought to enhance their status through trade or raids on rival settlements. In their acquisitive zeal and their obsession with rank—epitomized by ceremonies called potlatches at which titleholders defined their status through lavish gift giving—these tribal leaders had much in common with the ambitious foreigners who came to their shores. Like their European counterparts, the headmen could drive hard bargains. And, because they were dealing with not a single faction but several, they quickly learned how to play one off against another. As a result, they often trafficked with white men from a position of strength, if not outright superiority.

The pattern was set in 1778 when Captain James Cook entered an inlet on the west coast of Vancouver Island during the last of his three

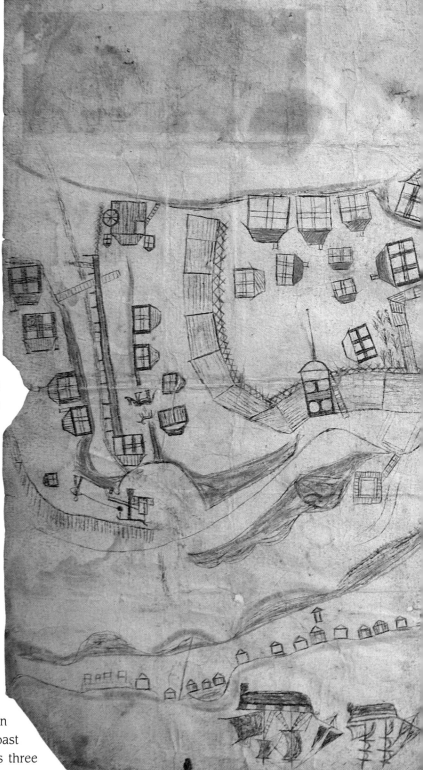

This rare view of a European outpost through native eyes shows Sitka, capital of Russian Alaska, around 1860. Russian buildings such as the cathedral and governor's mansion (upper right) loom large compared to the compact, colorless Indian dwellings (lower left), set off by a stockade.

epic voyages. A Spanish ship under Juan Pérez had anchored in the area four years earlier, but it had departed without landing because Pérez feared treachery from Indians who paddled out to greet him. Cook, by contrast, was anxious to repair and refit his two ships, and his experience with native cultures had taught him to distinguish between friendly and hostile gestures. Approaching in dugout canoes, Indians signaled their peaceful intentions. Several of them stood up one by one to speak in their local tongue, inviting the visitors to come ashore with bewildering words but intelligible gestures. One of the Indians sang "a very agreeable air," noted Captain Cook, "with a degree of softness and melody that we could not have expected."

Cook dubbed these cordial people the Nootka—a loose rendering of the name of their main coastal settlement as he heard it. The village was actually called Yuquot, and Indians had been living there for thousands of years during the spring and summer while passing the stormy months at more sheltered sites inland. The Nootka likewise defined the white men in terms of their habitation, referring to the visitors as *mamathni*, or "their houses move over the water." The Nootka had a sense of property that baffled the visiting Englishmen. The locals, Cook wrote, "were as light-fingered as any people we had before met with." They seemed to feel that their historic right to salvage whatever drifted ashore—including prized fragments of iron from wrecked ships—applied to anything not nailed down on Cook's vessels, a practice the English called stealing. The Nootka were miffed, in turn, when the English ignored the fact that everything around, including the stones on the beach and the grass underfoot, belonged to the tribe. When Cook ordered some of his men to cut hay around Yuquot to feed to the livestock he carried on board, Indians demanded payment. Cook complained that every blade of grass seemed to have a separate owner.

As this incident underscored, the Nootka knew how to get full value for things others wanted from them. They had sharpened their skills through centuries of intertribal barter and now took delight in a kind of daily bazaar with the Englishmen. In exchange for sea otter skins, fresh fish, and other commodities, they demanded more than beads and other diverting items. They wanted metals, especially iron to supplement their existing stock, which they hammered into points for their weapons or chisels and knives for shaping their intricately crafted canoes and long plank houses. One of Cook's crew, William Bayly, observed that the Nootka were "always asking for more, give them what you would." When Cook departed after one month's stay, the Nootka assembled in their canoes to sing farewell, proudly brandishing the more valuable items they had obtained from their guests in trade.

Cook had little idea of the value of the sea otter pelts he carried away, since the Russians had kept secret their trade with the Chinese. When his expedition reached China, his men were astonished to receive the equivalent of up to $120 per pelt. Official word of the riches to be had around Nootka Sound was delayed until the appearance of Cook's journals in 1784, five years after his death on the island of Hawaii. The publication launched a new fur rush, bringing scores of trading ships—first the English, whom coastal Indians dubbed "King George men," and then the "Boston men" from the infant American republic.

The influx of English speakers alarmed not only the Russians but also the Spaniards, who were anxious to protect their foothold in California and buttress their claims farther north. In 1789 they established an outpost at the village of Yuquot, temporarily dislodging the Nootka, and began seizing rival trading ships in the surrounding waters. The fort, whose garrison included descendants of the Inca from the Spanish colony in Peru, was abandoned six years later when the Spaniards concluded that their forces were inadequate to stifle the competition.

A picture of a three-masted vessel inscribed by a Nootka Indian on a rock on the shore of Vancouver Island expresses the fascination of the Indians with the huge sailing ships that began visiting the area in the late 1700s. Plied with gifts of canvas from eager white traders, expert native mariners emulated what they called "flying canoes" by fitting their own small craft with sails.

Traders from England and the United States were content for now to carry away furs and let the Indians be. During the 1790s, ships from these two countries hauled off to China some 100,000 sea otter pelts. By 1800 American firms dominated the trade, accounting for nearly nine of every 10 vessels visiting the British Columbia coast. A typical voyage from the East Coast took up to three years. After the journey around Cape Horn, the Boston men usually arrived in the late spring or summer, stopped at an inlet long enough to trade with Indians who paddled out to their ship, then moved on to another bay. Ships often wintered in Nootka Sound—where the sailors dubbed one harbor Friendly Cove in honor of the amicable residents—then spent a second summer of trade along the coast before sailing for China.

At first, some tribes were so eager to trade that they played into the visitors' hands. In 1787 an Englishman who stopped at the Queen Charlotte Islands reported that the Indians there—who called themselves the Haida, or the "people"—quarreled with each other "about which should sell his cloak first. Some actually threw their furs on board if nobody was at hand to receive them." Inhabitants of one village traded away 200 pelts for an equal number of iron chisels, worth a tiny fraction of what the furs would fetch. Such tools so impressed the Haida that they called the white visitors *Yets-haida,* or "iron people."

But as ships appeared with increased frequency, the Indians grew shrewder at trading. Besides iron chisels, they accepted copper in the form of kettles. Considering the metal too precious to be used for cooking, the Indians cut the kettles into bracelets and earrings. They generally refused "glasses, beads, and other baubles," as one visitor put it, and slighted what beads they did acquire by offering "them to us in derision."

Some traders were driven to feats of improvisation to satisfy the demanding Indians. In 1791 Captain Joseph Ingraham reached the Queen Charlotte Islands from Boston with a cargo of iron rods meant for conver-

A Makah Indian chief stands in his ornate canoe after calling on Spanish ships in Neah Bay, near the northwest tip of present-day Washington State. The Spaniards, who founded a settlement here in 1792, allowed only chiefs to board their vessels, fearing violence and what one Spaniard called the Indians' "inclination toward theft."

sion to chisels, only to discover that two British vessels had beaten him there with similar cargo and filled the need. Recalling the pattern of a copper bracelet he had seen on a Haida woman, he had the ship's blacksmith forge the rods into necklaces. The resulting ornaments weighed nearly five pounds, but the Haida loved them and snapped them up for the hefty price of three sea otter skins each. Another captain learned that some coastal Indians wore elk hides as armor to repel arrows and obtained a supply at favorable terms from Chinook Indians along the Columbia River. A third trader noticed that the Indians were enchanted by European clothing, which they coveted not to wear but to exchange in potlatches as tokens of status. The trader brought in a load of full-dress uniforms, and when they were gone, bartered all the extra clothing on board and ordered his sailmaker to fashion garments from spare canvas. Elsewhere, this same entrepreneur found Indians who delighted in crockery, and promptly traded most of the ship's cups and bowls.

Such flair for catering to the desires of coastal tribes sometimes took an unsavory turn. A few Boston traders served as middlemen in a regional slave trade, obtaining captives from accomplished warriors such as the Kwakiutl and offering them to tribes that had gained less by their raids on rivals. And captains catered so shamelessly to the Indian appetite for firearms that muskets became mediums of exchange along with woolen blankets—prized because they were warmer or more readily available than the mantles local tribes wove from plant fibers or animal fur. The value of a prime sea otter pelt, for example, might be pegged at three muskets or six wool blankets.

So intent were captains on pleasing their trading partners that most allowed Indians to come aboard to barter despite the obvious risks. Many traders also observed the widespread native custom of ceremonial gift exchange as a prelude to bargaining. One present they offered to coastal chiefs was a rigging of rudimentary sails for their canoes—a practice that introduced the sailboat to the coastal cultures. Alcohol also helped lubricate the wheels of commerce. After an initial Indian revulsion against liquor of all kinds, rum became extremely popular; a ship might carry up to 1,500 gallons of rum for presents and barter. The Tlingit liked rum so much that some began to distill their own from molasses taken in trade.

Although alcohol sometimes dulled their trading skills, Indians were seldom outbargained by the shrewd Yankees. As one captain put it, the locals proved to be "well versed in the tricks of the trade." To drive up the price of their pelts, he added, they would stroke the fur and extol its virtues or "go from one vessel to another, and back again, with assertions of offers made to them, which have no foundation." Time was on their side. They could afford to loll about the decks or wait alongside in their canoes for days on end, until the captain, whose livelihood depended on filling his hold with furs during the summer season, met their price.

Chiefs so powerful that they held neighboring villages in thrall found other ways of gaining advantage in the fur trade. They might prevent those neighbors from trading with the visitors, or snap up furs from them at a bargain and pass the pelts on to the white man at a premium. When short of stock, they might urge captains to wait while they gathered more pelts from their neighbors, even if that meant going to war to get them.

After such raids, the Nootka and other groups sometimes preserved the severed hands or skulls of their defeated rivals as trophies, leading white traders to conclude that the coastal Indians practiced cannibalism. This myth persisted despite an experiment conducted by one of the first visitors to Nootka Sound, Lieutenant John Williamson of Cook's expedition, who could not induce an Indian warrior to eat the flesh of a slain enemy even by tempting him with a small fortune in iron and brass. Despite the fierce reputation of the locals, few serious clashes occurred between the Indians and the whites along the British Columbia coast. Both sides benefited from the trade and thus had a vested interest in avoiding violence. Populous Indian communities stocked with firearms seldom felt threatened by the appearance of a visiting ship with a few dozen men aboard. And since many ships returned to the same anchorage, most captains were anxious to avoid offending the local tribe.

Even so, violence sometimes erupted. Many of the visitors subscribed to the dictum recorded in one sailor's log: "I believe it is impossible to keep friends with savages any longer than they stand in fear of you." Frustrated by shrewd Indian trading practices or acts of theft, captains

Wide-eyed faces stare like captured spirits from the bodies of a shorebird called an oystercatcher (center) and two fish on this fringed blanket woven in part from rare mountain goat wool, obtained by the Nootka through trade with the Kwakiutl of the British Columbia coast. Such blankets were worn on special occasions by heads of households, one of whom exchanged this prize with Captain Cook when he visited Nootka Sound in 1778.

occasionally resorted to tactics of the sort used by the Russians. They seized furs, took chiefs hostage, and even bombarded villages with cannon. In 1790 the Boston captain John Kendrick became enraged when the Haida persisted in stealing articles from his ship. To teach them a lesson, he captured their chief, Koyah, flogged him, cut off his hair, and confiscated many of his pelts. The humiliation cost Koyah prestige and demotion to lesser status by the tribe. When Kendrick returned the next year, Koyah had not forgotten. He led a futile attack on the ship that cost the lives of many of his warriors and further deflated his reputation. Unrepentant, Koyah later mounted unsuccessful assaults on other visiting vessels.

Of the Indians who lashed out against white traders, none gained more notoriety than the Nootka leader Maquinna. Soon after Cook's arrival in 1778, Maquinna, then in his twenties, succeeded his father as head of the highest-ranking household in Yuquot. Traditionally among the Nootka and other coastal peoples, the chief of the leading household was acknowledged by other family heads as first among equals and governed in consultation with them. White traders preferred to reckon with

A detailed portrait by Spanish artist José Cardero memorializes an Indian chief encountered on the eastern shore of Vancouver Island. His conical hat is adorned with a tassel in place of the peak favored by other chiefs (opposite).

one man, however, and their presence increased the wealth and status of chiefs such as Maquinna relative to other local leaders.

Reflecting his importance, Maquinna met the captains who anchored in Nootka Sound in a long cloak of sea otter fur and ceremonial makeup so ornate it took more than an hour to apply. "His complexion was of a dark copper hue, though his face, legs, and arms were so covered with red paint that their natural color could scarcely be perceived," noted John Jewitt, a young Briton serving as a blacksmith on the American ship *Boston* when its captain ran afoul of Maquinna in 1803. "His eyebrows were painted black in two broad stripes like a new moon, and his long black hair, which shone with oil, was fastened in a bunch on the top of his head and strewed or powdered all over with white down."

During a quarter-century of dealing with white captains, Maquinna and his people had amassed a tinderbox of grievances. One visitor had robbed him of 40 pelts; another had killed his second-ranking subaltern; yet another had replied to the theft of a chisel by firing on canoe loads of Nootka, killing more than 20 people. All this lent weight to a seemingly minor dispute that arose when the captain of the *Boston,* John Salter, gave Maquinna a double-barreled fowling gun as a present. Soon after receiving the gift, Maquinna returned to the ship, having broken a hammer on the weapon, and pronounced it defective. Salter—who was as proud as Maquinna when it came to the protocol of gift giving—reacted angrily, calling Maquinna a liar, among other epithets. As Jewitt commented, Maquinna knew English well enough to catch the drift of Salter's words, and he repressed his rage by

At top, Tatoosh— leader of the Indians who inhabited the island of that name near Neah Bay—wears a chief's hat decorated with a whaling scene in another study by Cardero, who also portrayed Tatoosh's principal wife and swaddled child.

repeatedly drawing his hand from his throat to his chest: "This, he afterwards told me, was to keep down his heart, which was rising into his throat and choking him."

The next day, Maquinna came out to the ship again with a large party of men, seemingly in high spirits. "He had a whistle in his hand and over his face a very ugly mask of wood, representing the head of some wild beast," reported Jewitt. "Whilst his people sang and capered about the deck, entertaining us with comic tricks and gestures, he blew his whistle to a kind of tune that seemed to regulate their motions." After putting the crew at ease, Maquinna told the captain that salmon were running in Friendly Cove and invited the sailors to take their fill. Salter dispatched his chief mate and nine men.

With the ship's crew divided, Maquinna ordered his warriors to attack. Brandishing daggers, axes, and clubs, they cut down Salter and the men around him in short order and sent a war party to slay the sailors who were fishing. Of the crew of 27, only the blacksmith Jewitt and a sailmaker named Thompson survived. Appreciative of their skills, Maquinna claimed the two as slaves. He also took the booty from the ship. In the days to come, he staged potlatches to burnish his prestige by distributing the muskets and other prizes to subordinates in Yuquot and to neighboring chiefs.

For Jewitt and Thompson, it was only the start of a long and bewildering ordeal. Word of the massacre reached white traders through native channels, and the captains kept their ships at a distance. With no immediate hope of deliverance, the captives' only recourse was to do Maquinna's bidding. Thompson fashioned a sail for Maquinna's canoe, while Jewitt forged a steel harpoon that the chief used to take a whale. "A great feast of the blubber was given at Maquinna's house," Jewitt related. "I was highly praised for the goodness of my harpoon and a quantity of blubber given me. I boiled it in salt water with some young nettles and other greens for Thompson and myself, and we found it tolerable food.'' After the feast, some of Maquinna's kinsmen asked Jewitt to make steel harpoons for them as well. ''But Maquinna would not permit this,'' the blacksmith recalled. ''He reserved this improved weapon for himself.''

Over time, the chief grew increasingly attached to the handy Jewitt and prevailed on him to adopt native dress and wed a high-ranking Nootka woman—whose dowry included two slaves who made Jewitt's life easier when he was not toiling for his own master. Jewitt found his wife ''amiable and intelligent,'' but never resigned himself to the forced match. ''Maquinna perceived this. He finally told me that if I did not like living with my wife, and that was the cause of my being so sad, I might part with her. I readily accepted this proposal, and the next day Maquinna sent her back to her father.'' Soon after, Jewitt, who suffered from the cold in his loose Nootka mantle, persuaded the chief to let him revert to European dress, thus ending his symbolic adoption into the tribe.

Wearing a majestic robe of sea otter fur, the legendary Nootka chief Maquinna entertains European guests in his spacious cedar lodge at the village of Yuquot. As portrayed at right in his whaler's hat in 1791—a dozen years before he seized the fur ship Boston and did away with most of its crew— Maquinna was a proud and cunning man who knew how to disguise his hostile intentions until he was ready to strike.

Caxique Pral. de Nutca nombrado Maquinna

Finally, after two years, Jewitt and Thompson were rescued by the Boston brig *Lydia,* whose captain lured Maquinna aboard and held him hostage until the sailors were freed. In the chief's presence, Jewitt argued against punishing him for the slaughter of the *Boston*'s crew. Jewitt said the attack resulted from Salter's insult and "the unjustifiable conduct" of earlier shipmasters. In any case, he added, any blow to the Nootka would only recoil on the next crew who stopped there. The captain of the *Lydia* agreed and made peace with Maquinna by exchanging his greatcoat for the Indian's mantle. Four months later, after trading in the north, the *Lydia* stopped again at Nootka Sound, where Jewitt visited amicably with Maquinna. "He was much pleased with his reception, inquiring how many moons it would be before I should come back to see him," Jewitt wrote. "He also told me that my Indian wife had borne me a son, and that he would send for him and take care of him as his own."

Over the next few decades, the focus of the fur trade in the Northwest shifted inland from the coast. By the 1820s, the sea otter had been hunted to near extinction, and merchants were trafficking in furbearing forest dwellers such as the river otter, beaver, marten, and mink. Soon white settlers infiltrated British Columbia and the Oregon Territory. These newcomers were less agreeable to Indian demands, and their incursions disrupted tribal ways and increased the toll of disease.

Yet the native peoples of the Northwest proved to be remarkably resilient. They had harnessed European technology to their needs. Indeed, such proud emblems as the totem poles that adorned many villages were made with the white man's tools. In the same accommodating spirit, tribes assimilated the offspring of diverse groups who had dallied on their shores. The blood of Russians, Spaniards, Englishmen, and Yankees mingled with that of Aleut, Koniag, Nootka, and other coastal peoples. And the genetic infusion was not limited to whites. Trading ship crews sometimes included Asians and Africans—who made their own contributions to the New World's rich racial blend and whose progeny, like Jewitt's son, were embraced by Native Americans as their own.

A COMMON GROUND OF TRADE

With steel adzes and chisels obtained in trade, the native artisans of the Northwest could work wood on a scale never possible before. After the arrival of trading ships, huge poles bearing clan or family crests (above and left) proliferated along the coast.

Over the course of generations beyond counting, the peoples of the Northwest Coast attuned themselves to the rhythmic changes of the sea—the surging tides, the coming of the salmon, the seasonal shift from bright days to storm and fog. But during the second half of the 18th century, the sea brought a change that was more profound than any they had ever known: From beyond the horizon came ships—primarily Russian, British, and American—in search of any riches the region might offer. Native and newcomer studied each other in some bafflement. The British explorer James Cook, who put into a Vancouver Island inlet in 1778, marveled as a reception party of Indians ceremoniously threw feathers and red dust toward his ships; the Indians kept a polite distance, conversing about the strangers and singing a song they thought appropriate to the occasion.

Even though contact between the two groups would lead to horrors of warfare and disease, there did exist some common ground for them. Like the mariners from across the ocean, the coastal Indians were practiced traders, eager to barter furs for metal tools, guns, and woven fabrics. Ironically, one consequence of acquiring foreign goods was a reaffirmation of longstanding native traditions. In myriad ways, Indian artists and craftsmen made vigorous use of the novel materials and implements as they portrayed supernatural beings and their links with humans. As seen in the creations sampled here and on the following pages, trade could enrich an ancient belief system even as it shaped a new reality.

178

EXTENDING THE ARTISAN'S RANGE

As materials from foreign sources came into their hands, Indian artisans incorporated them into their ancient creative repertoire and also used them to extend their expressive range. They discovered, for example, that metal could lend a new brightness to an eagle's eye *(left)*. Iridescent mother-of-pearl buttons—unknown before the white traders arrived—could be attached to a wool blanket to form a ceremonial robe *(below)* that flashed in the firelight when spirit beings were honored during traditional winter rites.

Brass buttons acquired from the Russians served as the eyes for a wooden Tlingit war helmet carved in the form of an eagle. The locks of hair affixed to the helmet may have come from enemy scalps.

Stitched to a dark blue wool trade blanket bordered with red flannel, gleaming rows of mother-of-pearl buttons shape a frog crest on this Tlingit robe. Crest-adorned blankets had been worn by dancers since ancient times; the so-called button blanket became the standard version in the 19th century.

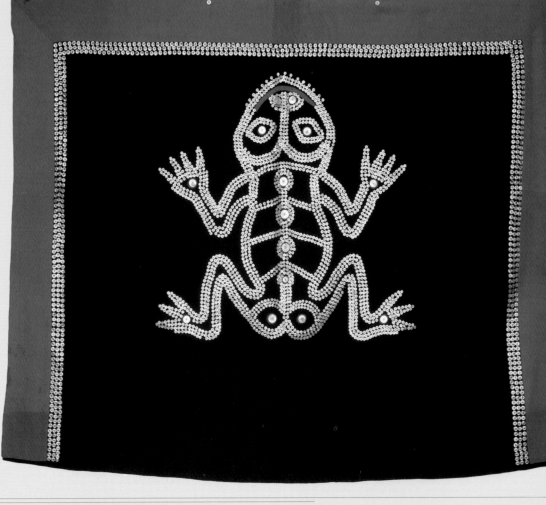

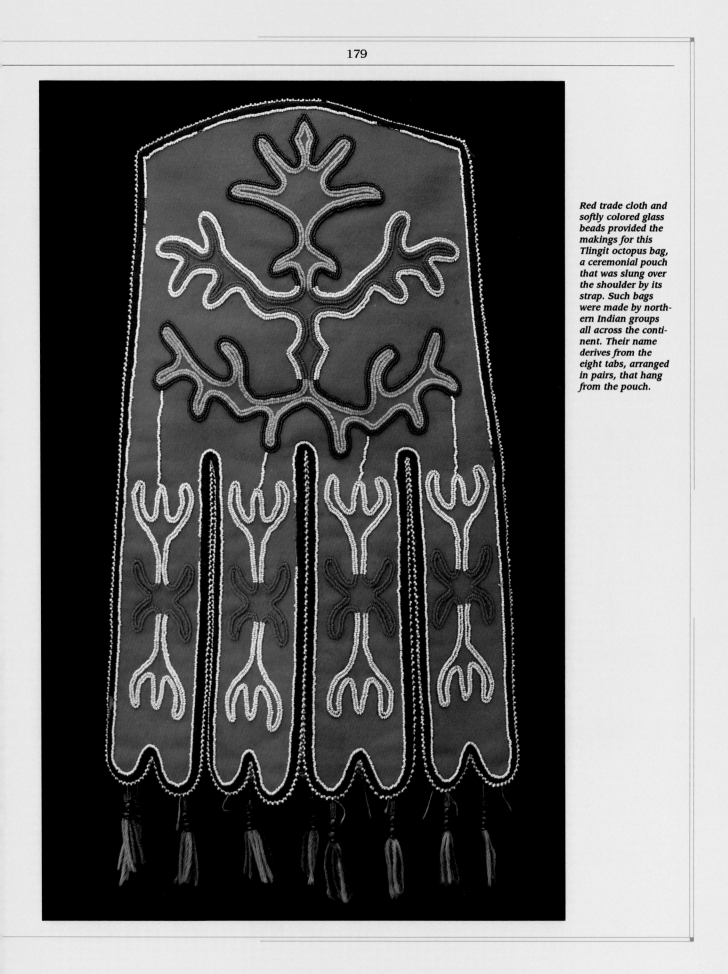

Red trade cloth and softly colored glass beads provided the makings for this Tlingit octopus bag, a ceremonial pouch that was slung over the shoulder by its strap. Such bags were made by northern Indian groups all across the continent. Their name derives from the eight tabs, arranged in pairs, that hang from the pouch.

MASTERING NEW METALS

Indian smiths had long fashioned native copper into weapons and other articles, and they quickly adapted to the iron, steel, and silver that were introduced by the whites. Much of their metalwork was created in accordance with traditional forms, but there were departures as well. A gun barrel, for example, could be turned into the bowl of a pipe for tobacco smoking—a European-inspired practice that replaced the local custom of sucking pellets made from a mixture of dried tobacco and lime.

The wooden hilt of this sheathed dagger is topped by a totemic image combining a man and an eagle. Adorned with abalone-shell inlays, the pommel was carved from walnut, a wood of foreign origin taken from the stock of a discarded musket. Steel from a sword, bayonet, or butcher's knife was reworked in order to make the blade.

Engraving skills practiced on copper or such organic materials as goat horn and antler were increasingly used to create gold or silver ornaments, such as this silver bracelet bearing the ancient motif of a dogfish.

A section of the iron barrel of a worn-out musket provided the bowl for this Tlingit pipe, decorated with abalone inlays and human hair. A hollow shoot was inserted in the base to serve as the pipestem.

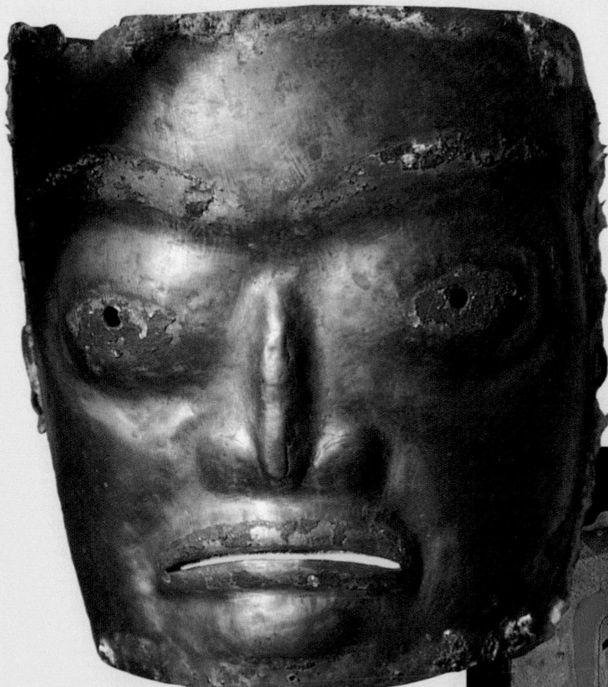

A ceremonial mask made entirely of copper attested to its owner's wealth. The metal was a significant item of barter, highly valued for its brilliance and warm color.

A bear crest adorns this shirt made of elk hide, a tough material eagerly sought by northern coastal groups for use as armor. White traders obtained the hides from Indian villages near the mouth of the Columbia River and along the Juan de Fuca Strait.

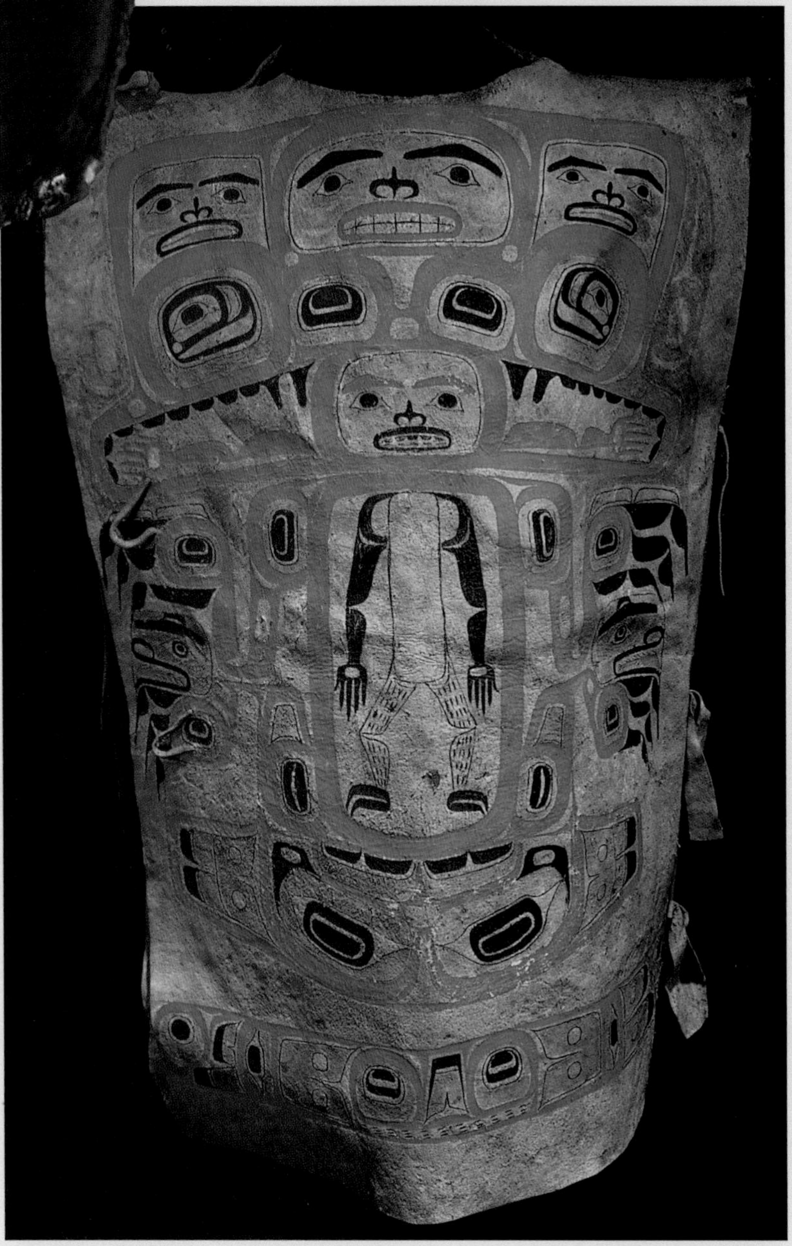

BARTERING IN NOVEL WAYS

Just as aristocrats in distant lands craved the lustrous fur of the Pacific Coast sea otter, high-ranking Indians in the Northwest prized the white pelts of ermine. Because native ermine were scarce, an eager market developed for imported skins. All-fur deals were arranged; in 1804, for example, an American trader accepted 500 sea otters for 2,500 ermine skins that had originated in Germany. The newcomers also became middlemen between Indian groups, obtaining elk hides *(right)* from southern peoples and exchanging them for sea otter pelts in the north. At the same time, they largely preempted the long-established Indian copper trade, supplying sheets of the metal for use in objects ranging from jewelry to masks.

Ermine skins amplify the sumptuous effect of a ceremonial headdress worn by a dancing chief in the Pacific Northwest. Additional embellishments include swanskin, split baleen, buckskin, and abalone shell.

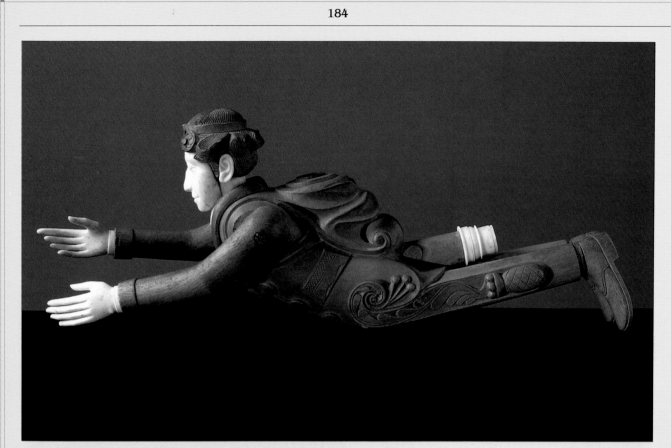

Fashioned of walrus ivory and walnut that had been taken from a gun-stock, this figurehead-like pipe is modeled on a ship's officer.

DESIGNING FOR EXPORT

Like good traders anywhere, the Indians of the Northwest studied their white counterparts closely and began creating articles mostly for export. Some of these items were rooted in the past; the hat at right, for example, was a new version of the headgear that the Indians had worn for centuries to keep off the sun and rain. Many of the articles exploited a material rarely used before—a soft black shale called argillite, which could be easily carved into curios that appealed to the tastes of the foreigners.

Inspired by the look of a 19th-century sailor's cap, this basket hat was made for trade. Indian artisans could produce headgear of any shape and decorative pattern, weaving the hats with split spruce or sometimes cedar bark.

Argillite, a mineral whose sole source was a mountainside in the Queen Charlotte Islands, was shaped into a huge assortment of export goods, from platters (above) to curios depicting Yankee sea captains (right).

ACKNOWLEDGMENTS

The editors wish to thank the following individuals and institutions for their valuable assistance:

In Canada:
Quebec—Chris Kirby, Canadian Museum of Civilization, Hull.

In the Dominican Republic:
Santo Domingo—Bernardo Vega, Fundación Dominicana.

In Italy:
Bergamo—Mario Guerra, Museo Scienze Naturali "E. Caffi." Rome—M. A. Fugazzola, Donatella Saviola, Museo Nazionale L. Pigorini.

In Russia:
Saint Petersburg—The Museum of Anthropology and Ethnography, Kuntzkamer, Russian Academy of Science; The Repin Academy of Fine Arts.

In Spain:
Madrid—Araceli Sanchez Garrido, Museo de América.

In Sweden:
Bålsta—Intendent Bengt Kylsberg, Weapons Museum, Skoklosters Slott.

In the United States:
California: Oakland—Randy Millikin. San Juan Capistrano—Nicholas Magalousis, Mission San Juan Capistrano Museum. Santa Barbara—John Johnson, Museum of Natural History.

Maine: Augusta—Ed Churchill, Maine State Museum.

Massachusetts: Salem—Jeffrey Brain, Peabody Museum.

New Mexico: Pecos—Ann Rasor, Linda L. Stoll, Pecos National Historical Park. Santa Fe—Arthur Olivas, Donna L. Pierce, Willow Powers, Richard Rudisall, Cordelia Snow, Louisa Stivers, Museum of New Mexico.

Virginia: Williamsburg—Thomas E. Davidson, Stephen Furey-Moore, Donald C. Garland, Deborah Padgett, Matthew E. Riddick, Stephen B. Simons, Jamestown-Yorktown Foundation.

Washington State: Kirkland—David Storie. Seattle—Rebecca Andrews, The Burke Museum, University of Washington; Laura Kearney, Paul M. Macapia, Seattle Art Museum; Richard H. Engeman, University of Washington Libraries; Sari Ott, Stan Shockey, University of Washington.

BIBLIOGRAPHY

BOOKS

Ammannati, Francesco, et al., *Bologna e il Mondo Nuovo.* Bologna, Italy: Grafis Edizioni, 1992.

Axtell, James, *After Columbus: Essays in the Ethnohistory of Colonial North America.* New York: Oxford University Press, 1988.

Aztecs: Reign of Blood & Splendor, the Editors of Time-Life Books (Lost Civilizations series). Alexandria, Va.: Time-Life Books, 1992.

Bancroft-Hunt, Norman, *People of the Totem: The Indians of the Pacific Northwest.* New York: Peter Bedrick Books, 1989.

Berkh, Vasili, *The Chronological History of the Discovery of the Aleutian Islands or the Exploits of the Russian Merchants: With the Supplement of Historical Data on Fur Trade.* Transl. by Dimitri Krenov. Seattle: Works Progress Administration, 1938.

Bezy, John V., and Joseph P. Sanchez, eds., *Pecos—Gateway to Pueblos & Plains: The Anthology.* Tucson: Southwest Parks and Monuments Association, 1988.

Billard, Jules B., ed., *The World of the American Indian.* Washington, D.C.: National Geographic Society, 1989.

Bourne, Edward Gaylord, ed., *The Voyages and Explorations of Samuel de Champlain.* Transl. by Annie Nettleton Bourne. 2 vols. New York: Allerton Book Co., 1922.

Bowden, Henry Warner, *American Indians and Christian Missions: Studies in Cultural Conflict* (Chicago History of American Religion series). Chicago: University of Chicago Press, 1981.

Casas, Bartolomé de las:
The Devastation of the Indies: A Brief Account. Transl. by Herma Briffault. New York: Seabury Press, 1974.
History of the Indies. Ed. and transl. by Andrée Collard. New York: Harper & Row, 1971.

Cook, Sherburne F., *The Conflict between the California Indian and White Civilization.* Berkeley: University of California Press, 1976.

Damas, David, ed., *Arctic.* Vol. 5 of *Handbook of North American Indians.* Washington, D.C.: Smithsonian Institution, 1984.

Drucker, Philip, *Cultures of the North Pacific Coast.* San Francisco: Chandler Publishing, 1965.

Duff, Wilson, *The Impact of the White Man.* Vol. 1 of *The Indian History of British Columbia.* Victoria, British Columbia: Provincial Museum of Natural History and Anthropology, 1964.

Feest, Christian F., *The Powhatan Tribes.* New York: Chelsea House Publishers, 1990.

Fisher, Robin, *Contact and Conflict: Indian-European Relations in British Columbia, 1774-1890.* Vancouver: University of British Columbia Press, 1977.

Fisher, Robin, and Hugh Johnston, eds., *Captain James Cook and His Times.* Seattle: University of Washington Press, 1979.

Fitzhugh, William W., and Aron Crowell, *Crossroads of Continents: Cultures of Siberia and Alaska.* Washington, D.C.: Smithsonian Institution, 1988.

Hackett, Charles Wilson, ed., *Revolt of the Pueblo Indians of New Mexico and Otermín's Attempted Reconquest, 1680-1682.* Glendale, Calif.: Arthur H. Clark, 1942.

Hallenbeck, Cleve, *Land of the Conquistadores.* Caldwell, Idaho: Caxton Printers, 1950.

Hauptman, Laurence M., and James D. Wherry, eds., *The Pequots in Southern New England: The Fall and Rise of an American Indian Nation.* Norman: University of Oklahoma Press, 1990.

Heizer, Robert F., ed., *California.* Vol. 8 of *Handbook of North American Indians.* Washington, D.C.: Smithsonian Institution, 1978.

Holm, Bill:
The Box of Daylight: Northwest Coast Indian Art. Seattle: Seattle Art Museum and University of Washington Press, 1983.
Spirit and Ancestor: A Century of Northwest Coast Indian Art at the Burke Museum. Seattle: University of Washington Press, 1987.

Howay, Frederic W., ed., *Voyages of the "Columbia" to the Northwest Coast, 1787-1790 and 1790-1793.* Boston: Massachusetts Historical Society, 1941.

Hudson, Charles M.:
The Juan Pardo Expeditions: Exploration of the Carolinas and Tennessee, 1566-1568. Washington, D.C.: Smithsonian Institution Press, 1990.
The Southeastern Indians. Knoxville: University of Tennessee Press, 1976.

Hulton, Paul, *America 1585: The Complete Drawings of John White.* Chapel Hill: University of North Carolina Press, 1984.

Hunt, William R., *Arctic Passage: The Turbulent History of the Land and People of the Bering Sea, 1697-1975.* New York: Charles Scribner's Sons, 1975.

Jennings, Francis, *The Ambiguous Iroquois Empire: The Covenant Chain Confederation of Indian Tribes with English Colonies from its Beginnings to the Lancaster Treaty of 1744.* New York: W. W. Norton, 1984.

Jennings, Francis, et al., eds., *The History and Culture of Iroquois Diplomacy: An Interdisciplinary Guide to the Treaties of the Six Nations and Their League.* Syracuse: Syracuse University Press, 1985.

Jewitt, John R., *The Adventures and Sufferings of John R. Jewitt: Captive of Maquinna.* Seattle: University of Washington Press, 1987.

John, Elizabeth A. H., *Storms Brewed in Other Men's Worlds.* College Station: Texas A & M University Press, 1975.

Joppien, Rüdiger, and Bernard Smith, *The Voyage of the "Resolution" and "Discovery," 1776-1780.* Vol. 3 of *The Art of Captain Cook's Voyages.* New Haven: Yale University Press, 1988.

Judd, Carol M., and Arthur J. Ray, eds., *Old Trails and New Directions: Papers of the Third North American Fur Trade Conference.* Toronto: University of Toronto Press, 1980.

Kerr, Robert, *A General History and Collection of Voyages and Travels, Arranged in Systematic Order: Forming a Complete History of the Origin and Progress of Navigation, Discovery, and Commerce, by Sea and Land, from the Earliest Ages to the Present Time.* Edinburgh: William Blackwood, 1824.

Kessell, John L., *Kiva, Cross, and Crown: The Pecos Indians and New Mexico, 1540-1840.* Washington, D.C.: National Park Service, 1979.

Knuth, Egil, *Aron of Kangek: The Norsemen and the Skraelings.* Godthaab, Greenland: Det Gronlandske Forlag, 1968.

Krell, Dorothy, ed., *The California Missions: A Pictorial History.* Menlo Park, Calif.: Lane Publishing, 1979.

Kupperman, Karen Ordahl, *Roanoke: The Abandoned Colony.* Totowa, N.J.: Rowman & Allanheld, 1984.

Levenson, Jay A., ed., *Circa 1492: Art in the Age of Exploration.* Washington, D.C.: National Gallery of

Art, 1991.

Makarova, Raisa V., *Russians on the Pacific, 1743-1799*. Ed. and transl. by Richard A. Pierce and Alton S. Donnelly. Kingston, Ontario: Limestone Press, 1975.

Masterson, James R., and Helen Brower, *Bering's Successors, 1745-1780*. Seattle: University of Washington Press, 1948.

Milanich, Jerald T., and Susan Milbrath, eds., *First Encounters: Spanish Explorations in the Caribbean and the United States, 1492-1570*. Gainesville: University of Florida Press, 1989.

Morison, Samuel Eliot, *The Maritime History of Massachusetts, 1783-1860*. Boston: Houghton Mifflin, 1921.

New England Begins: The Seventeenth Century. Vol. 1. Boston: Museum of Fine Arts, 1982.

Ogden, Adele, *The California Sea Otter Trade, 1784-1848*. Berkeley: University of California Press, 1941.

Oswalt, Wendell H., *Eskimos and Explorers*. Novato, Calif.: Chandler & Sharp Publishers, 1979.

Quinn, David B.:
Explorers and Colonies: America, 1500-1625. London: Hambledon Press, 1990.
North America from Earliest Discovery to First Settlement. New York: Harper & Row, 1977.
Set Fair for Roanoke: Voyages and Colonies, 1584-1606. Chapel Hill: University of North Carolina Press, 1985.

Quinn, David B., ed., *New American World: A Documentary History of North America to 1612*. Vols. 1, 2, 3, and 5. New York: Arno Press, 1978.

Rawls, James J., *Indians of California: The Changing Image*. Norman: University of Oklahoma Press, 1984.

Russell, Howard S., *Indian New England before the Mayflower*. Hanover, N.H.: University Press of New England, 1980.

Sabo, George, III, and William M. Schneider, eds., *Visions and Revisions: Ethnohistoric Perspectives on Southern Cultures*. Athens: University of Georgia Press, 1987.

Salisbury, Neal, *Manitou and Providence: Indians, Europeans, and the Making of New England, 1500-1643*. New York: Oxford University Press, 1982.

Shelikhov, Grigorii I., *A Voyage to America, 1783-1786*. Ed. by Richard A. Pierce, transl. by Marina Ramsay. Kingston, Ontario: Limestone Press, 1981.

Silverberg, Robert, *The Pueblo Revolt*. New York: Weybright and Talley, 1970.

Simmons, William S., *The Narragansett*. New York: Chelsea House Publishers, 1989.

Soft Gold: The Fur Trade & Cultural Exchange on the Northwest Coast of America. Portland: Oregon Historical Society, 1990.

Spicer, Edward H., *Cycles of Conquest: The Impact of Spain, Mexico, and the United States on the Indians of the Southwest, 1533-1960*. Tucson: University of Arizona Press, 1962.

The Spirit Sings: Artistic Traditions of Canada's First Peoples. Toronto: McClelland and Stewart, 1987.

Suttles, Wayne, ed., *Northwest Coast*. Vol. 7 of *Handbook of North American Indians*. Washington, D.C.: Smithsonian Institution, 1990.

Terrell, John Upton, *Pueblos, Gods and Spaniards*. New York: Dial Press, 1973.

Thomas, David Hurst, ed.:
Archaeological and Historical Perspectives on the Spanish Borderlands West. Vol. 1 of *Columbian Consequences*. Washington, D.C.: Smithsonian Institution Press, 1989.
Archaeological and Historical Perspectives on the Spanish Borderlands East. Vol. 2 of *Columbian Consequences*. Washington, D.C.: Smithsonian Institution Press, 1990.
Ethnology of the Indians of Spanish Florida. New York: Garland Publishing, 1991.
The Missions of Spanish Florida. New York: Garland Publishing, 1991.
Spanish Borderlands Sourcebooks. New York: Garland Publishing, 1991.

Thornton, Russell, *American Indian Holocaust and Survival: A Population History since 1492*. Norman: University of Oklahoma Press, 1987.

Tikhmenev, P. A., *A History of the Russian-American Company*. Ed. and transl. by Richard A. Pierce and Alton S. Donnelly. Seattle: University of Washington Press, 1978.

Treasures. Hull, Quebec: Canadian Museum of Civilization, 1988.

Trigger, Bruce G.:
The Children of Aataentsic: A History of the Huron People to 1660. Kingston, Ontario: McGill-Queen's University Press, 1987.
The Impact of Europeans on Huronia. Vancouver, British Columbia: Copp Clark Publishing, 1969.
Natives and Newcomers: Canada's "Heroic Age" Reconsidered. Kingston, Ontario: McGill-Queen's University Press, 1985.

Trigger, Bruce G., ed., *Northeast*. Vol. 15 of *Handbook of North American Indians*. Washington, D.C.: Smithsonian Institution, 1978.

Ubelaker, Douglas H., and John W. Verano, eds., *Disease and Demography in the Americas*. Washington, D.C.: Smithsonian Institution Press, 1992.

Udall, Stewart, *In Coronado's Footsteps*. Tucson: Southwest Parks and Monuments Association, 1991.

Viola, Herman J., *After Columbus*. Washington, D.C.: Smithsonian Institution, 1990.

Walker, Alexander, *An Account of a Voyage to the North West Coast of America in 1785 & 1786*. Ed. by Robin Fisher and J. M. Bumsted. Vancouver, British Columbia: Douglas & McIntyre, 1982.

Washburn, Wilcomb E., ed., *History of Indian-White Relations*. Vol. 4 of *Handbook of North American Indians*. Washington, D.C.: Smithsonian Institution, 1988.

Webb, Edith Buckland, *Indian Life at the Old Missions*. Lincoln: University of Nebraska Press, 1982.

Wellman, Paul I., *Glory, God and Gold: A Narrative History*. Garden City, N.Y.: Doubleday, 1954.

Wheeler, Keith, and the Editors of Time-Life Books, *The Alaskans* (The Old West series). Alexandria, Va.: Time-Life Books, 1977.

Wilbur, C. Keith, *Early Explorers of North America*. Chester, Conn.: Globe Pequot Press, 1989.

Wilson, Samuel M., *Hispaniola: Caribbean Chiefdoms in the Age of Columbus*. Tuscaloosa: University of Alabama Press, 1990.

Wood, Peter H., Gregory A. Waselkov, and M. Thomas Hatley, eds., *Powhatan's Mantle: Indians in the Colonial Southeast*. Lincoln: University of Nebraska Press, 1989.

Wroth, Lawrence C., *The Voyages of Giovanni da Verrazzano, 1524-1528*. New Haven: Yale University Press, 1970.

PERIODICALS

Blakely, Robert L., "A Coosa Massacre." *Archaeology*, May/June 1989.

Blakely, Robert L., and Bettina Detweiler-Blakely, "The Impact of European Diseases in the Sixteenth-Century Southeast: A Case Study." *Midcontinental Journal of Archaeology*, 1989.

Blakely, Robert L., and David S. Mathews, "Bioarchaeological Evidence for a Spanish-Native American Conflict in the Sixteenth-Century Southeast." *American Antiquity*, 1990.

Boyd, Mark F., "The Arrival of De Soto's Expedition in Florida." *The Florida Historical Quarterly*, 1938.

Dye, David H., "Death March of Hernando De Soto." *Archaeology*, May/June 1989.

Guest, Francis F., "An Examination of the Thesis of S. F. Cook on the Forced Conversion of Indians in the California Missions." *Southern California Quarterly*, Spring 1979.

Hickerson, Harold, "Fur Trade Colonialism and the North American Indian." *The Journal of Ethnic Studies*, Summer 1973.

Hudson, Charles, et al., "Coosa: A Chiefdom in the Sixteenth-Century Southeastern United States." *American Antiquity*, 1985.

Martin, Calvin, "The European Impact on the Culture of a Northeastern Algonquian Tribe: An Ecological Interpretation." *The William and Mary Quarterly*, January 1974.

McGhee, Robert, "Contact Between Native North Americans and the Medieval Norse: A Review of the Evidence." *American Antiquity*, 1984.

Milanich, Jerald T., "Hernando De Soto and the Expedition in Florida: An Overview." *The Florida Anthropologist*, December 1989.

Miller, Christopher L., and George R. Hamell, "A New Perspective on Indian-White Contact: Cultural Symbols and Colonial Trade." *The Journal of American History*, September 1986.

Quimby, George I.:
"Culture Contact on the Northwest Coast, 1785-1795." *American Anthropologist*, April-June 1948.
"Japanese Wrecks, Iron Tools, and Prehistoric Indians of the Northwest Coast." *Arctic Anthropology*, 1985.

Ronda, James P., " 'We Are Well As We Are': An Indian Critique of Seventeenth-Century Christian Missions." *The William and Mary Quarterly*, January 1977.

Snow, Dean R., and Kim M. Lanphear, "European Contact and Indian Depopulation in the Northeast: The Timing of the First Epidemics." *Ethnohistory*, Winter 1988.

OTHER PUBLICATIONS

Davidson, Thomas E., "Powhatan's Mantle." Williamsburg, Va.: Jamestown Settlement.

Hedrick, Basil C., and Carroll L. Riley, "The Journey of the Vaca Party: The Account of the Narváez Expedition, 1528-1536, as Related by Gonzalo Fernández de Oviedo y Valdés," University Museum Studies No. 2. Carbondale: Southern Illinois University, 1974.

PICTURE CREDITS

The sources for the illustrations that appear in this book are listed below. Credits from left to right are separated by semicolons, from top to bottom by dashes.

Cover: Giraudon, Paris. **6, 7:** Fil Hunter, courtesy Jamestown-Yorktown Educational Trust, Jamestown Settlement, Williamsburg, Virginia—print collection of the Miriam and Ira D. Wallach Division of Art, Prints and Photographs, The New York Public Library, Astor, Lenox and Tilden Foundations. **8:** Map by Maryland CartoGraphics, Inc. **10:** Courtesy Bernardo Vega—Musée de l'Homme, Paris. **11:** Archivio Fotografico, Soprintendenza Speciale al Museo Nazionale L. Pigorini, Rome. **12:** From the Florentine Codex by Bernardino de Sahagún, copied by Donato Pineider/Biblioteca Medicea-Laurenziana, Florence. **14:** © Lee Boltin. **15:** Robert S. Oakes, © 1972 National Geographic Society. **16:** Giraudon, Paris. **17:** Archiv für Kunst und Geschichte, Berlin—Giraudon, Paris. **18:** Giraudon, Paris. **19:** Lauros-Giraudon, Paris. **22:** Map by Maryland CartoGraphics, Inc.—Jeffrey M. Mitchem, Parkin, Arkansas; Robert R. Allen, Norwood, Louisiana. **23:** Photograph courtesy Florida Division of Historical Resources, Bureau of Archaeological Research—David H. Dye, Memphis State University, Tennessee. **24:** Bildarchiv Preussischer Kulturbesitz, Berlin, courtesy Staatsbibliothek, Augsburg. **25:** Robert L. Blakely/Georgia State University, Atlanta. **27:** Bildarchiv Preussischer Kulturbesitz, courtesy Kunstbibliothek, Berlin. **28, 29:** Luis Arenas, Archivo General de Indias, Seville; courtesy The New York Historical Society, New York City, neg. no. 69413. **33-36:** Courtesy Trustees of the British Museum, London. **38:** G. Dagli Orti, Paris. **39:** Private collection, Jamestown-Yorktown Foundation, Jamestown Settlement, Williamsburg, Virginia. **40:** Library of Congress, neg. no. USZ62-73206. **41:** Ashmolean Museum, Oxford. **42:** Map by Maryland CartoGraphics, Inc. **43:** Courtesy Virginia Department of Historic Resources, from the Hand Site, Southampton County—courtesy Virginia Department of Historic Resources, Saint George Collection (2)—courtesy Dr. Stephen R. Potter and Dr. Diane E. Gelburd, all photographed by Fil Hunter at Jamestown Settlement, Williamsburg, Virginia. **44:** National Portrait Gallery, Washington, D.C./Art Resource, New York; Fil Hunter, courtesy Jamestown-Yorktown Educational Trust, Jamestown Settlement, Williamsburg, Virginia. **45:** Fil Hunter, courtesy Jamestown-Yorktown Educational Trust, Jamestown Settlement, Williamsburg, Virginia. **47:** Fototeca Storica Nazionale, Milan. **48, 49:** Background Fil Hunter; Fil Hunter, courtesy Jamestown-Yorktown Foundation, Jamestown Settlement, Williamsburg, Virginia. **50-53:** Fil Hunter, courtesy Jamestown-Yorktown Foundation, Jamestown Settlement, Williamsburg, Virginia. **54, 55:** Musée de l'Homme, Paris, Cl. M. Delaplanche—The Huntington Library, San Marino, California. **57:** Canadian Museum of Civilization, Hull, Quebec, neg. no. S89-1831. **58:** Smithsonian Institution, Washington, D.C., neg. no. 56,827. **59:** Map by Maryland CartoGraphics, Inc. **60, 61:** Courtesy the John Carter Brown Library at Brown University, Providence (2). **62:** The Historical Society of Pennsylvania—Peabody Museum of Salem, Massachusetts, photograph by Mark Sexton. **63:** Photo-

graph courtesy New York State Museum, Albany. **64, 65:** Smithsonian Institution, Washington, D.C., neg. no. 75-6012. **66, 67:** The New York Public Library, Astor, Lenox and Tilden Foundations. **69:** Hudson's Bay Company Archives, Provincial Archives of Manitoba, Winnepeg. **70, 71:** © Longeville, l'Agence PUBLIPHOTO, Montreal, Quebec. **72:** Department of Ethnography, The National Museum of Denmark, Copenhagen. **73:** National Archives of Canada, Ottawa, Ontario, neg. no. C-5750. **74, 75:** Paintings by John Verelst, courtesy National Archives of Canada, Ottawa, Ontario, neg. nos. C-92414; C-92418; C-92416; C-92420. **76:** Peabody Museum of Salem, Massachusetts, photograph by Mark Sexton. **77:** Rare Books and Manuscripts Division, The New York Public Library, Astor, Lenox and Tilden Foundations. **78:** Library of Congress, neg. no. USZ62-32055. **80:** Smithsonian Institution, Washington, D.C., neg. no. 840-A—property of Massachusetts Historical Society, photograph by Mark Sexton. **81:** Collection of the Boston Athanaeum, photograph by Mark Sexton. **82:** National Museum of the American Indian, Smithsonian Institution, Washington, D.C., photo. nos. 4662—4663. **84-91:** Department of Ethnography, The National Museum of Denmark, Copenhagen, photographs by Kit Weiss. **92, 93:** © David Muench. **94, 95:** Background © Lawrence Ormsby. George H. H. Huey; Ann Rasor, Pecos National Historical Park, New Mexico (2). **96, 97:** George H. H. Huey—courtesy Abell-Hanger Foundation and Permian Basin Petroleum Museum, Midland, Texas; © Abell-Hanger Foundation. **98, 99:** Background © Lawrence Ormsby. George H. H. Huey; Ann Rasor, Pecos National Historical Park, New Mexico (2). **100, 101:** © Tom Till; Museum of New Mexico, Santa Fe, neg. no. 2604. **102:** Courtesy Elisabeth Waldo-Dentzel Collection, Multicultural Arts Studios Northridge, California. **104:** Polly Schaafsma. **106, 107:** © Jerry Jacka; courtesy the Librarian, Glasgow University Library, Scotland. **108:** The British Library, London, Harley MS.3450, folio 10. **109:** Private collection, courtesy Patricia Janis Broder, *Shadows on Glass: The Indian World of Ben Wittick* by Patricia Janis Broder, Rowman and Littlefield, Savage, Maryland, 1990. **110:** Map by Maryland CartoGraphics, Inc. **111:** DeGolyer Library, Southern Methodist University, Dallas, reproduced from *The Bison* in *Art* by Larry Barsness, Northland Press, Flagstaff, Arizona, 1977. **112, 113:** Museum of New Mexico, Santa Fe, neg. no. 73903. **114:** © Jerry Jacka, courtesy Arizona State Historical Society. **116, 117:** Baker Aerial Photography; © Jerry Jacka. **118:** Rare Books and Manuscripts Division, The New York Public Library, Astor, Lenox and Tilden Foundations. **120:** © Jerry Jacka. **122, 123:** Rare Books and Manuscripts Division, The New York Public Library, Astor, Lenox and Tilden Foundations. **124, 125:** Museum of Indian Arts and Culture, Laboratory of Anthropology, Museum of New Mexico, Santa Fe, photographs by Blair Clark. **127:** © Jerry Jacka. **128, 129:** © Tom Till; © Jerry Jacka—George H. H. Huey; Laurence E. Parent. **130, 131:** Museum of New Mexico, Santa Fe, neg. no. 86305—Museum of International Folk Art, Museum of New Mexico, Santa Fe, photograph by Blair Clark. **132:** Palace of the Governors, Museum of New Mexico, Santa Fe, photographs by Blair Clark. **133:** Ben Benschneider, courtesy Museum of New Mexico, Santa Fe. **135:** Museum of New Mexico, Santa Fe. **136, 137:** Cour-

tesy The Bancroft Library, Berkeley, California; map by Maryland CartoGraphics, Inc. **138:** Museo Naval, Madrid; courtesy The Bancroft Library, Berkeley, California (2). **140, 141:** Wm. B. Dewey, courtesy Santa Barbara Mission Archive-Library, California. **142, 143:** Henry Groskinsky, courtesy Mission San Miguel Arcángel, California; Ventura County Museum of History and Art, California—Henry Groskinsky, courtesy San Gabriel Mission, California. **144, 145:** The Huntington Library, San Marino, California; Santa Barbara Historical Society, California. **146:** From the Smithsonian Institution exhibition *Crossroads of Continents: Cultures of Siberia and Alaska,* courtesy the collections of The Museum of Anthropology and Ethnography, Saint Petersburg, Russia. **148:** Courtesy Trustees of the British Museum, London. **149:** Oregon Historical Society, OrHi 3559—Special Collections Division, University of Washington Libraries, Seattle, neg. no. UW13374. **150:** Map by Maryland CartoGraphics, Inc. **152, 153:** Peabody Museum, Harvard University, Cambridge, Massachusetts, photographs by Hillel Burger. **155:** Smithsonian Institution, Washington, D.C., neg. no. 37,212. **156, 157:** Special Collections Division, University of Washington Libraries, Seattle, photograph by Webster & Stevens—Smithsonian Institution, Washington, D.C., neg. no. 92-6461. **158:** Special Collections Division, University of Washington Libraries, Seattle, photographs by N. B. Miller, neg. nos. NA3049—NA3048. **160, 161:** Library of Congress—from the Smithsonian Institution exhibition *Crossroads of Continents: Cultures of Siberia and Alaska,* courtesy the collections of The Museum of Anthropology and Ethnography, Saint Petersburg, Russia. **162:** From the Smithsonian Institution exhibition *Crossroads of Continents: Cultures of Siberia and Alaska,* courtesy the collections of the R. E. Repin Institute of Painting, Sculpture and Architecture, Saint Petersburg, Russia. **164, 165:** V.D.11. Sheldon Jackson Museum, Sitka, Alaska, photograph by Sitka Rose Studio. **167:** Steve C. Wilson/Entheos, Seabeck, Washington State. **168, 169:** Museo de América, Madrid. **171:** Courtesy Trustees of the British Museum, London. **172, 173:** Museo Naval, Madrid. **174:** Oronoz, Foreign Ministry Archive, Madrid. **175:** Museo Naval, Madrid. **176, 177:** Werner Forman Archive, London. **178:** Seattle Art Museum, gift of John H. Hauberg, cat. no. 91.1.72, photograph by Paul Macapia—Thomas Burke Memorial Washington State Museum, cat. no. 1-1495, photograph by Eduardo Calderón. **179:** Seattle Art Museum, gift of John H. Hauberg, cat. no. 91.1.78, photograph by Paul Macapia. **180, 181:** Peabody Museum, Harvard University, Cambridge, Massachusetts, photographs by Hillel Burger (2); Seattle Art Museum, gift of John H. Hauberg, cat. no. 91.1.130, photograph by Paul Macapia—Thomas Burke Memorial Washington State Museum, cat. no. 2.5E561, photograph by Eduardo Calderón. **182:** Collection of Bill and Marty Holm, photograph by Paul Macapia. **183:** Werner Forman Archive, London/National Museum of Man, Ottawa, Ontario—Peabody Museum, Harvard University, Cambridge, Massachusetts, photograph by Hillel Burger. **184, 185:** Peabody Museum, Harvard University, Cambridge, Massachusetts, photographs by Hillel Burger (2); private collection, photographed by Paul Macapia; Thomas Burke Memorial Washington State Museum, cat. no. 25.0/286, photograph by Eduardo Calderón.

INDEX

Numerals in italics indicate an illustration of the subject mentioned.